1st Publication 2016
2nd Publication 2020
3rd Publication 2022

Cëgullah Publishing & Apologetics Academy
International Copyright © 2023
www.cegullahpublishing.ca
All rights reserved.

Watching, Waiting, Warning Course Consists of 3 books:
1-Textbook: Commission & Orders   978-1-926489-80-3
2-Prayerbook: Tactics & Weaponry   978-1-926489-81-0
3-Workbook: Bootcamp & Early Training   978-1-926489-82-7

Cover photo © iStock 1190807747
Cover design by Jeanne Metcalf.

COPYRIGHT MATTERS

This book is an original manuscript by the author, protected by **international copyright** laws of Canada. Therefore, no part of this author's work may be reproduced, in part or in whole, or stored in a retrieval system, or transmitted in any form or by any means, electronic, mechanical, photocopied, recorded or otherwise for commercial use without the *prior written* permission of the author. However, ***it is possible to receive permission*** to use short quotations for personal use, or use in a group study, or for permission to copy certain passages, or to make portions of the writings available for overhead viewing. Simply, contact Cegullah Publishing[1] to request it.

SCRIPTURE MATTERS

All scripture quotes originate from KJV, public domain. However, the name of God most often appears as **YeHoVaH or YHVH not LORD**. *See the Appendix of the* **textbook** *for more information about this substitution*[2].

---

[1] Cegullahpublishing.ca

[2] In this book, we often refer to the day of the LORD. Because this is a well-known term, we did not change LORD to YHVH

This Bible Study consists of 3 books:

Book #1 -Textbook
Commission & Orders
5.5" x 8.5"

Book #2 -Prayer Book
Tactics & Weaponry
5.5" x 8.5"

Book #3. Workbook
Boot Camp & Early Training
8.5" x 11"

TABLE OF CONTENTS

COURSE 403
SECTION 1: UNARMED & ILL-EQUIPPED

CHAPTER		
	Introduction..	23
1	Unarmed?..	37
2	Why Armed?...	53
3	Why Change?..	71

SECTION 2: ARMED AND READY

WATCHING:

4	Targeted Recruitment	101
5	Tactical Training..	125
	Prayer Book Assignment.........................	143

COURSE 404
(Section 2 continued)
WAITING

6	Targeted Solutions..................................	151
7	Tactical Avoidances.................................	173
	Prayer Book Assignment.........................	194

WARNING:

8	Targeted Surveillance.............................	199
9	Tactical Responses.................................	215
	Prayer Book Assignment.........................	229
	Conclusion..	233

APPENDIX

Cegullah Publishing...	242
Hebrew Alphabet..	237
Scriptural Reference...	239

TO STUDENTS IN THE DEGREE PROGRAM

This workbook, like its accompanying textbook, holds 2 Courses.

1. **Course 403 includes Section 1 & part of Section 2.**
   When finished the textbook there is a Prayer Book assignment.
   In Course 403, the instructions follow Chapter # 5, just prior to moving on to Course 404.

Before moving on, be sure you complete the following:
   - Submit the required reports.
   - Write the exam at the end of this Section.
     - You must have 69% Grade to receive the credit hours.
     - You must have 75% Grade to continue to the next course.

NOTE: This course is worth 6 credits towards your degree.

2. **Course 404 is Sections 2 to the end.**
   When finished the textbook there are 2 Prayer Book assignments. One after Chapter 7, and one after Chapter 9.

When finished, be sure you complete the following:
   - Submit the required reports.
   - Write the exam at the end of this Course.
     - You must have 69% Grade to receive the credit hours.
     - You must have 75% Grade to continue to the next course.

NOTE: This course is worth 6 credits towards your degree

COURSE GRADING

This Grading applies to Course 403 and 404

SPECIFICS OF DEGREE GRADING	%
Online Course Audio Completion Acknowledgement	7
Course Completion Acknowledgement	2
Workbook Completion Acknowledgement	5
Workbook Chapter Reviews	12
Prayer book Reviews	6
Section Review Form	12
Personal Testimony of your spiritual benefit from this course	8
All of the above must be submitted before scheduling the final exam	52
Online Course Final Exam	48
TOTAL	100
Passing Grade to receive credits	69
NOTE: Grade to continue taking courses for your degree	75

All forms are found online.

TO UNACCREDITED STUDENTS:

If you are studying unaccredited, we invite you to do all the exercises in the workbook, however, your study does not require the submission of reports or exams. Therefore, please overlook the messages regarding Course numbers, and information on the requirements at each section end. Simply move on to the next section.

We pray that as you do your homework, and perhaps, review your answers with others, that your roots in God will go down deep as you unravel the truths of the scriptures.

May God richly bless you.

TO ALL STUDENTS:

ALWAYS BEGIN EVERY COURSE WITH THE WORKBOOK!

Every course that we at Cegullah Publishing & Apologetics Academy designs, we write to present the student with an inductive style environment. Thus, students
Have opportunity for learning scriptures, first, on their own before we teach them. We do this because we believe every person who desires to learn God's Word can do so by prayerfully reading scriptures, by seeking the Holy Spirit for insight, and then, by reading the accompanying textbook to help keep the student on the right track. So, unless otherwise advised within the workbook, keep the textbook closed and only open after finishing that particular chapter.

HOW TO SPIRITUALLY BEGIN EVERY LESSON

Step # 1: **IMPORTANT:**
Before you begin your study, take some time with YeHoVaH to prepare your heart to receive whatever He wishes to share with you. Do this every time you approach the workbook or read the textbook. In this way, you will make this time a deeply personal time of fellowship between you and your Heavenly Father, YeHoVaH!

A NOTE FROM THE AUTHOR

Many years ago, in an effort to better understand Income Tax, I took a course on how to prepare personal returns. At that time, the teacher made a blatant statement giving his listening audience a key to success: "Learn to read," he said, "follow the instructions and you will do well." He went on to explain that from his experience, students often skimmed the contents of the page, and thus, overlooked the steps giving them the simple instructions.

As a result, some students gave up preparing income tax, considering the job and its detailed entries, overwhelming. Other students, in a hurry to make money by doing returns, rushed with the forms, and inevitably missed entries or deductions. These made too many errors, which resulted in too much time spent going back over the forms to fix the problems.

As the teacher continued his talk, he went on to say he knew the key to success in income tax preparation. He said, "it rests in one's ability to *read the text and do what it says*".

This advice works well in the study of scripture, too.

DOING THE WORKBOOK

In this workbook, you will find many scriptures. Following the scripture, you will discover several questions about that scripture passage. Each question has a purpose. That purpose is to help you gain an understanding of the text. The secret to understanding the text rests in your ability to literally, *hear*[3] the words of the text. Therefore, as you answer the questions, use as much wording from the scripture as possible. ***Please do not add your opinion or even what you have been taught earlier about that passage.*** Approach each passage fresh. Simply answer the questions using the

---

[3] This is one reason why the Jews always read the text out loud.

wording of the scripture under study[4]. Why this may seem a redundant process, in the long run, it helps you learn.

HOW TO ANSWER FROM THE TEXT

John 14:6	
Jesus saith unto him, I am the way, the truth, and the life: no man cometh unto the Father, but by me.	
Question	Who is speaking in verse 6?
Answer	**Yeshua (Jesus)**
Question	What 3 things did Yeshua say about Himself?
Answer	**I am the way, the truth, and the life.**
Question	Through Whom does a person come?
Answer	**Yeshua**
Question	To Whom does a person come?
Answer	**to the Father**

Each question asked helped to break up the basic components of the passage, thus positioning the reader to understand more. This works with simple passages like John 14:6, and it works with more complicated passages, too. With larger portions of scripture, repeated readings may be necessary, and thus, reinforce the truth.

To study scripture, please remember these points:
59. **Always begin with prayer**. Use the Bible Study to intensify and escalate your relationship with the Almighty.
60. **Spend time praying about any passage**. Should you find you do not understand it, ask the Holy Spirit to guide you to unlock the truth. While commentaries can be helpful and sometimes clarify difficult passages, please do not make them your first place of investigation. Pray and ask God to show you, first. Then, investigate.
61. **Look at passages set in their original language**. At times, certain passages require a little more clarity, so they must be considered within their original language and cultural setting. (e.g., Hebraic

---

[4] Most students find this a little hard to do, however, in the long run this habit reaps great rewards.

scriptures (First Covenant[5]) or Apostolic Scriptures (Second Covenant). To do that, find a good online bible program that gives you the root word. Using KJV makes looking up the root words easy, since Strong's Exhaustive Concordance co-relates nicely with the KJV.

62. **Keep passages within their original setting.** When reading the text in the Chapters, if the passage is not familiar to you, go to your Bible and read the passage within its setting of chapter and book.

63. **Be honest in answering any personal questions asked.** If studying in a group and asked to share, if your answer seems too personal or difficult to share, simply tell the teacher that you prefer to pass on this one.

64. **Encourage yourself when needed.** Whenever you encounter Chapters requiring lots of time, or you feel overwhelmed, take some time to pray and think about the passages. Remember the old riddle asked to a young child: "How do you eat an elephant?". Remember the answer: one bite at a time! Thus, approach long Chapters by answering one question at a time until finished. To benefit from scripture at any time in your life, "read the text (scriptures) and do what it says". In that, you will find fulfilment in your God and your faith, confident how to live it out, victoriously.

"**Be doers and not hearers only of the Word of God**" [6]

65. **Time constraints**:
    - *Accredited students*, consider doing the homework by meting it out in a daily allotment. You might consider an hour or two a day.
    - *Unaccredited students*, split your time in doing your study as best suits your schedule.

No matter how you decide to do your homework, remember, the idea is not to see how quickly you can get it done. Rather, use the workbook as a tool to get to know the Word and its author better.

Hopefully, understanding these few terms will keep us on the same page!

---

[5] The book of Hebrews, when referring to the Hebraic written scriptures, refers to them as the First Covenant.
[6] Based on James 1:22

Before closing this note, please understand that your primary goal to study God's Word is to get to know the God of the Bible. This comes, slowly, as you read the Bible and prayerfully connect with Him. To put it another way, you intentionally take time to study His Word, reading it slowly with faith, knowing that the Holy Spirit helps you learn its meaning. To do so brings forth fruit which produces *life* in you for God's Word are Spirit and life! That life produces evidence that you have been with God! It is a valuable treasure deposited in your life, which otherwise does not come to you!

Beloved, do not be content just to listen to others teach, expound, or present His Word to you! Study it for yourself!

In light of your faith walk with God, dear reader, there is nothing more powerful, inspiring, or rewarding than connecting with God through His Living Word, *a category in which the written Word falls.*

Dear one, I realize we lead busy lives, some more busy than others. However, time management becomes paramount when connecting with God, and His Word must take an important priority. Prayerfully, ask God to help you, faithfully and consistently study His Word. Ask Him if you need to set some other thing aside in order to give the Word of God the priority in your life that He desires. Freeing your time to study the Word brings with it such a rewarding satisfaction as He blesses you for your determination to know His Word and learn of Him and His ways.

Please consider these helps as you move forward to read, study, grow and connect with the Living God!

Richest blessings.
Jeanne

Jeanne Metcalf – President and CEO
Cegullah Publishing & Apologetic Academy Inc.
www.cegullahpublishing.ca

COURSE OPENING INFORMATION

ORIGINAL BIBLE TRANSCRIPTS

Since God gave the Bible to His People in a language, other than English, it is important for those English-speaking people studying the Bible to understand that God guaranteed Divine Inspiration in the original transcripts, not in English Bible translations. Ardent Bible students need to realize that fact and then look at the original transcripts of the Bible for clarity, but not everyone has the education to do that. Thus, over the years, scholars prepared materials for the average person to use as an aid to understand the meaning of the original words. One of the best sources is Strong's Exhaustive Concordance[7]. Its author identified all the root words of the Hebraic Scriptures and Apostolic Scriptures, assigned a number to each word, and then gave a broad explanation of that word in English to help students understand the original message the word conveyed.

One further aid to understanding the original transcripts comes from a recent discovery by scholars who uncovered the original pictograph language used in ancient times. This discovery further expands the original concept of the Hebrew Words. While the basic meaning of many of those Hebrew words may not be even identical to Modern Hebrew, it does open our understanding to grasp some concepts of its ancient meaning and gives a broader view of the deeper things in the Word of God.

Since this book often refers to the Ancient Pictograph Language, we include here a short explanation on that language for the reader to review. It is in no way a complete study but is merely an overview to help the student grasp the concept of the ancient picture language and explains why it is used in this book.

---

[7] This book was first published in 1890 and is available for purchase at most Christian bookstores. It is also available for use in computer format.

THE ANCIENT PICTURE LANGUAGE

Whenever you translate something from one language to another, there is always a risk of compromising the depth of the original language, especially if that language is not as expressive as the original, and does not hold words, which precisely articulate the meaning. Such is the case when translating from Hebrew to English. For example, to translate a Hebrew 'tallit', which is an important part of the traditional Jewish garment, worn by men, we have no such English word to express it. The word tallit means, "little tent", but the translators simply interpreted it as tent. In our language, however, when we think of a tent, we know there are large tents and pup tents. However, 'tallit', if properly interpreted, is, in reality, a woven shawl traditionally made on a white background, in which people wrap themselves when they are in prayer alone with God. Today we call that a "prayer shawl". Translating the word, 'tallit' as 'tent', hardly means the same thing.

This is but one instance where early interpretations of scripture erred, and because of that one little mistake, many believers think that Acts 18:3, that described the Apostle Paul as abiding with 'tentmakers', means that Paul made tents, meaning outdoor shelters, when in fact, as a trained Pharisee, Paul made prayer shawls. This is but one instance but there are many other places in the Word, where translators overlooked cultural expressions and the like, and thus, gave the reader a different meaning than the original transcripts.

We must always ensure, when looking at Hebrew words with our English mind, that we consider these things and remember that *Hebraic thinking differs greatly from our Western world.* Differences in thinking, between Hebraic and Western thought, would take a lot of time to explain, so for now, keep in mind, that the Hebraic language is 'relational' while the Western World is not. The Hebrew picture language explains that point well.

AN AGRICULTURAL, RELATIONSHIP-BASED LANGUAGE

The early Hebrew language, like other languages, began as an *agriculturally based language* explaining ideas of their civilization with 'pictures' relative to their environment. The alphabet, in this early language, was comprised of letters, whose design indicated certain parts of the body to describe certain words. Other letters used well-known animals, such as the ox and others, to describe common things during their civilization's existence. For example, the letter "aleph", the first letter, pictured an ox's head, and the second letter "bet" represented a tent where the family lived. To explain this in further detail, we will look at the word, "father", which uses both the "aleph" and the "bet".

THE HEBREW WORD FOR FATHER

Hebrew words usually have a base of three characters. The first two characters are known as Parent Root, the characters following are known as the Child Root. [8] The word for father is "Ab". In English as you can see, there are two letters, A and b. In the Hebrew, in this case, there are also two letters, but they are not A and b, but ALEPH and BET. In order to read the Hebrew, there is something you must remember and that is the direction in which to read Hebrew.

In English, we read this way ⟶ from Left to Right,
In Hebrew, we read this way ⟵ from Right to Left.

For us, this seems rather awkward, but nevertheless, keep that in mind as you read the letters below.

BET   ALEPH

In the picture language, an Ox's head represents the Aleph, and the Bet is pictured as a dwelling place, or a tent. The **ox** is a strong animal, used to pull carts and carry heavy burdens and the like. Within a tent, the family lived. Putting this together, you have a picture of a strong person, capable

---

[8] When understanding "Parent and Child Root" it is only in the most simplistic format that it is easy to interpret. Past four or five characters, it is more difficult to grasp.

of carrying burdens, caring for the family. Hence, the Hebrew picture language describes the father as this: *The strong person over the family, or to put it another way, a father is the strong one of the house.*

Keep in mind that the pictograph language, in Hebrew, is relational, rather than abstract as in the English language. A study of it produces amazing thoughts from which we can learn much.

PROPER USE OF THE PICTURE LANGUAGE

Throughout this study, we will look at many Hebrew words in order to obtain a deeper meaning of the Word. As you learn some of those deeper meanings, please realize that you cannot automatically substitute that broader meaning of that word whenever you come across the same English word in the version of scripture that you read. When translating the Bible, scholars may have used the same English word for two or three different Hebrew words. For example, in the Hebrew Scriptures, we find two major words that mean peace. Once word is שלום, pronounced Shalom. This word is familiar to many of us. Expanding it to the ancient picture language, it means "to break every authority causing chaos". With the absence of chaos, the result is peace. The other Hebrew word is חרש, pronounced khaw-rash. This word, many do not know. Its picture in the ancient pictograph language suggests blocking words that come from the head, or in other words, it means speechless, to remain silent. Here again is a picture of peace, but not the same in context as the first word in Hebrew, nor of our idea of peace in English.

When looking at Hebrew words from the ancient, pictograph language, ensure that you observe some basic rules. Unless you are a Hebrew scholar, with a good understanding of sentence structure, only use the expanded meaning to apply to the immediate subject at hand. Also, ensure its meaning fits well within the context of other scriptures giving reference to the same topic.

If you follow these simple rules, you should do fine!

IMPORTANT INFORMATION ABOUT A STRONG`S CONCORDANCE.	
When using a concordance to look up Hebrew &Greek words remember:	
The Hebraic Scriptures (First Covenant):	written in Hebrew or Hebrew/Chaldean
The Apostolic Scriptures (New Covenant)	Are written in Koine Greek
When looking up these words in a Concordance, the following system is often used:	G plus the # = Greek Words e.g. G2875 H plus the # = Hebrew Words e.g. H2875 *some computers use a "0" rather than the H

Please note:

While this workbook is called Boot Camp & Early Training, additionally, there is an accompanying booklet entitled, Boot Camp Drills. That booklet holds helpful statements of faith and is free on our website.

Find it either with the QR code or by entering Boot Camp Drills into the search engine.

COURSE 403
WATCHING. WAITING. WARNING.

SECTION 1 –

Unarmed & Ill-equipped

INTRODUCTION[9]

In order to get the best out of any biblical material, it is always best to begin with prayer. If you have not already done so, please take some time and pray now, before you begin this Chapter. After prayer, please read the letter from Cegullah Publishing (pages 5 to 10). Record any pertinent information you might with to remember below.

---

[9] Note: Due to the way we designed this course, we felt it best to leave the introduction separate rather than combining it into the first chapter.

Please read the following pages, then answer the questions that immediately afterward.

BOOT CAMP

After the children of Israel were freed from slavery, Moses and the people sang this song:

> *"Then sang Moses and the children of Israel this song unto YeHoVaH, and spoke, saying, I will sing unto YeHoVaH, for he has triumphed gloriously: the horse and his rider has he thrown into the sea. The LORD is my strength and song, and he is become my salvation: he is my God, and I will prepare him a dwelling place; my father's God, and I will exalt him. The LORD is a man of war: Yahweh is his name."*[10]

Exodus 15:1-3

This passage, declaring the Lord as a man of war, is not an isolated passage! Both Hebraic and Apostolic scriptures have much to say about the might and power of God.

> *"Who is this King of glory? The LORD strong and mighty, YeHoVaH mighty in battle."*

Psalm 24:8 .

> *"Gird your sword upon your thigh, O most mighty, with your glory and your majesty. "*

Psalm 45:3

> *"And I saw heaven opened, and behold a white horse; and he that sat upon him was called Faithful and True, and in righteousness he does judge and make war. His eyes were as a flame of fire, and on his head were many*

---

[10] Deviation from King James Version in these scriptures are by the author.

> *crowns; and he had a name written, that no man knew, but he himself. And he was clothed with a garment dipped in blood: and his name is called The Word of God. And the armies which were in heaven followed him upon white horses, clothed in fine linen, white and clean. And out of his mouth goes a sharp sword, that with it he should smite the nations: and he shall rule them with a rod of iron: and he treads the winepress of the fierceness and wrath of Almighty God. And he has on his vesture and on his thigh a name written, KING OF KINGS, AND LORD OF LORDS."*
>
> *Revelation 19:11-16*

God, indeed, is a mighty warrior, and we His people are called to fight for His Kingdom. That battle, however, is not a physical battle where believers fight flesh and blood. Rather, it is a spiritual battle. Nevertheless, God desires His children to be equipped to face the battle. To those ends, He has given the believer all that is needed for victory. Paul, the Apostle, said this same thing, only in different words in his second letter to the Gentile converts at Corinth:

> *"Now I Paul myself implore you by the meekness and gentleness of Christ ... For though we walk in the flesh, we do not war after the flesh: (For the weapons of our warfare are not carnal, but mighty through God to the pulling down of strong holds;) Casting down imaginations, and every high thing that exalts itself against the knowledge of God, and bringing into captivity every thought to the obedience of Christ; And having in a readiness to revenge all disobedience, when your obedience is fulfilled. Do ye look on things after the outward appearance ..."*
>
> *2 Corinthians 10:1a, 3-7 a*

Words such as "weapons of warfare" denote a military application to a believer's life, ensuring the believer understands the warfare is against *a spiritual foe*. While many believers know these scriptures, some do not understand that, like a soldier in a war, we must live our life understanding the spiritual battle we face, how to face it, and how to be victorious. Far too many succumb to the wiles of the spiritual foe, often because they are not familiar with the militant way, in which God commands His people to live. Recapping that form of life and to show the disciplined mindset, Yeshua said, "Occupy till I come."[11]

For those who have a listening ear to the Holy Spirit, today, it seems clear that many believers do not understand their role as a soldier in the Kingdom of God, and frankly, many of them do not wish to embrace their role. Nevertheless, that role is given to us. God's army, however, does not come by conscription, but rather as a request for volunteers. Those who decide to back away and refuse to even watch over their own life, leave themselves vulnerable to deception through the wiles of ha satan. That adversary does not care who falls victim to his attacks! God, on the other hand, cares deeply for each and every person. He alone knows the number of casualties fallen to ha satan's wiles, and what's more, He knows what would have been prevented. If only His people obeyed the command of Yeshua to "watch and pray", so much would be different!

Yeshua knew what it meant to enter into a spiritual battle, yet, He learned to rest in His Father's victories. Even so, Yeshua knew how to "watch and pray" and He wanted His disciples, for their own good, to do so also. In addition, Yeshua expected that command to go forward in every generation. Somehow, it has been swept under the carpet. Forgotten! The effect of its neglect seems very evident in the Body of Messiah, today. Thus, this material, "Watching. Waiting. Warning" came into being. With its militant terms, such as "boot camp and early training", "commission and orders", "tactics and weaponry", its intentions are to present the command of Yeshua to watch and pray in such a manner as to ready the believer for the spiritual warfare and discipline which normally accompanies the Christian life. Also, should the believer decide to be a "watchman" for the Lord, watching over

---

[11] Luke 19:13 And he called his ten servants, and delivered them ten pounds, and said unto them, Occupy till I come.

the lives of others, it gives some important helps to point the believer in that direction.

"Boot Camp & Early Training" is where you, the believer, work the hardest. You get to dig into the Word of God. You get to put on your military armour in prayer. You get to stretch your spiritual muscles any way your personal training coach, the Holy Spirit, leads you. You get to see how other recruits are doing as you share your homework with others!

In between your training sessions, (times you meet to do your homework), you are called into a classroom setting to receive your "Commission and Orders", (your textbook). To ensure you are trained well, you are given some exercises using spiritual "tactics and weaponry". This the Prayerbook which holds information on the believer's arms, the believer's ally (which, by the way, is the believer's secret weapon), and the believer's armoury. Each section has solid biblical truth to strengthen its readers.

Finally, when finished boot camp and early training, you take your material with you into the real world. There you take up your post as a watchman, first, over your own life, and second, over the lives of others, as the Lord leads. In truth, there are valuable life-giving Chapters in the pages of these books! Use them to the best of your ability. Use them to pick up your shield of faith and stand with the many others God has called to the front lines of His Kingdom. Use them to advance the good news of His Kingdom. Use them to "occupy" until He comes!

Get ready now, to move into your part of the process! To complete the Introduction, answer the questions on the following pages.

INTRODUCTION QUESTIONS:

1. Why did you decide to take this study, entitled, "Watching. Waiting. Warning?"

2. What do you hope to gain from taking this study?

3. Without looking at a dictionary, and without getting theological at this point, write out, in a few words, definitions for the following words:

   1. Watching

   2. Waiting

   3. Warning

   4. Boot Camp

SECTION 1

4. What is the purpose of an army "Boot camp"?

5. Have you ever been to Boot camp? If so, describe what you experienced.

6. When Boot camp is over, what normally happens to the recruits: a) during war time, and b) during peace times?

During War Time	During Peace Time

Introduction

7. If someone finds Boot camp too difficult, how does the army handle it?

8. From what you know of the church today, is there anything militant about the church? Explain your answer.

9. From what you know of the early church, in the days of the book of Acts, was there anything militant about the church? Explain your answer. (If you wish to cite a passage of scripture to support your answer, please do so!)

10. In looking at the overall church (ekklesia) today, do you think there is a place for a more militant attitude? If so, please explain where and why?

   Where?

   Why?

11. Returning to the subject of the army, often they appoint sentries to stand guard at various places of entrance. For example, at times, sentries stand on guard in front of the entrance to our Parliament buildings in Ottawa. In the space below, write out some duties of a sentry.

12. What happens if a sentry falls asleep, leaves his post or decides to treat his job as boring?

13. Most businesses today have a security system in place. Without going into too much detail, highlight the operation of a normal alarm system.

14. From what you know of scripture, is there any form of spiritual alarm system that God gave the church? Explain your answer with supporting scripture.

In the book of Acts, the Apostle Paul came upon an altar. It read, "To the Unknown God"[12]. Paul used the knowledge of that altar to begin a conversation with an audience, and from that beginning, declare to them the name of that unknown God. Basically, Paul built his message on the base of something they knew. This is a good example for teachers to follow. Thus, this Chapter was set in place to *get you thinking,* as well as begin our study together on common ground. We'll build on that, from here on, beginning Chapter 1!

---

[12] Acts 17:23 For as I passed by, and beheld your devotions, I found an altar with this inscription, TO THE UNKNOWN GOD. Whom therefore ye ignorantly worship, him declare I unto you.

PRECIOUS MOMENTS RECAP

One goal of our academy is to help each student come away from an in-depth learning of scripture with a deeper, more intricate connection with the One, Who redeemed them. Afterall, it is through the Word of God that we begin to know about our God, and it is through that same Word that we understand how our God thinks. If we are to obey the scripture and to cleave to our God as Deuteronomy 11:22 tells us, then, we need to set in place certain specifics to do so.

> *Deuteronomy 11:22*
> *"For if ye shall diligently keep all these commandments which I command you, to do them, to love YHVH your God, to walk in all his ways, and to cleave (cling) unto him;"*

Therefore, to help you build on this connection with God, we ask that you review the chapter, looking for the scriptures that spoke to you the most. Record those scriptures in the box below along with why that scripture spoke to you. Additionally, as you review this workbook chapter, pull to the front of your thinking at least one spiritual truth that spoke to you.

We will call the last three questions, **PRECIOUS MOMENTS RECAP.**

PRECIOUS MOMENTS RECAP

15.	QUESTION:	Review this workbook chapter. Pick out the scriptures that spoke to you the most. Write at least one of those scriptures in the space below.
	ANSWER:	
16.	QUESTION:	What specific truth from the scriptures you studied in this workbook chapter speaks to you. Write that truth in the space below.
	ANSWER:	*(continue your answer here)*

SECTION 1

WATCHING. WAITING. WARNING.

Unarmed & Ill-Equipped

17.	QUESTION:	Think of how you can apply this scripture to your life. Enter those thoughts in the space below.
	ANSWER:	

CHAPTER 1 – Unarmed?

Read the following scriptures. As you do, you'll notice that, behind certain words, there are angular brackets behind a bolded word. Inside the brackets is a 4 or 5-digit number. Ignore that number for the time being. We'll come back to that number later.

Genesis 2:15 And YeHoVaH God took the man, and put him into the garden of Eden to dress it and to **keep <8104>** it.		
1.	Question:	What does this scripture tell us God did?
	Answer:	
2.	Question:	For what purpose did God do this?
	Answer:	

SECTION 1 — WATCHING. WAITING. WARNING. — Unarmed & Ill-Equipped

Genesis 17:9 And God said unto Abraham, Thou shalt **keep <8104>** my covenant therefore, thou, and thy seed after thee in their generations.		
3.	Question:	Verse 9 says God requires 2 things. List them.
	Answer:	1.
		2.

Exodus 15: 23 And when they came to Marah, they could not drink of the waters of Marah, for they were bitter: therefore the name of it was called Marah. 24 And the people murmured against Moses, saying, What shall we drink? 25 And he cried unto YeHoVaH; and YeHoVaH shewed him a tree, which when he had cast into the waters, the waters were made sweet: there he made for them a statute and an ordinance, and there he proved them, 26 And said, If thou wilt diligently hearken to the voice of YeHoVaH thy God, and wilt do that which is right in his sight, and wilt give ear to his commandments, and keep **<8104>** all his statutes, I will put none of these diseases upon thee, which I have brought upon the Egyptians: for I am YeHoVaH that healeth thee.		
4.	Comment:	In the journey from Egypt to the Promised Land, the children of Israel stopped for water at a place named "Marah". *(Marah means bitter.)*
	Question:	How did the children of Israel respond to Moses? (vs 24)
	Answer:	
5.	Question:	How did Moses respond? (vs 25)
	Answer:	
6.	Question:	How did the Lord respond to Moses? (vs 25)
	Answer:	

Chapter 1 — Unarmed?

7.	Question:	What does verse 25 say God made for the people?
	Answer:	
8.	Question:	What is the ordinance mentioned in verse 26?
	Answer:	
9.	Question:	What does the Lord promise to do, if Israel kept His commandments? (vs 26)
	Answer:	

Numbers 6: 22 ¶ And YeHoVaH spake unto Moses, saying, 23 Speak unto Aaron and unto his sons, saying, On this wise ye shall bless the children of Israel, saying unto them, 24 The LORD bless thee, and **keep <8104>** thee: 25 The LORD make his face shine upon thee, and be gracious unto thee: 26 The LORD lift up his countenance upon thee, and give thee peace. 27 And they shall put my name upon the children of Israel; and I will bless them.

10.	Comment:	This is known as the Aaronic blessing.
	Question:	Read verse 23. Why is this called the Aaronic blessing?
	Answer:	
11.	Question:	Why do you think God wanted it given to Aaron?
	Answer:	
12.	Question:	What 2 parts of the blessing are in verse 24?
	Answer:	

SECTION 1

WATCHING. WAITING. WARNING.

Unarmed & Ill-Equipped

13.	Question:	What 2 parts of the blessing are in verse 25?
	Answer:	
14.	Question:	What 2 parts of the blessing are in verse 26?
	Answer:	
15.	Question:	What does Moses say in verse 27?
	Answer:	
16.	Question:	Why do you think that Aaron was not allowed to use his own words to bless the people? (Hint: look at verse 27!)
	Answer:	

Deuteronomy 4:5 "**5** Behold, I have taught you statutes and judgments, even as YeHoVaH my God commanded me, that ye should do so in the

land whither ye go to possess it. **6 Keep (8104)** therefore and do *them*; for this *is* your wisdom and your understanding in the sight of the nations, which shall hear all these statutes, and say, Surely this great nation *is* a wise and understanding people. **7** For what nation *is there so* great, who *hath* God *so* nigh unto them, as YeHoVaH our God *is* in all *things that* we call upon him *for*? **8** And what nation *is there so* great, that hath statutes and judgments *so* righteous as all this law, which I set before you this day? **9** Only take **heed (8104)** to thyself, and keep thy soul diligently, lest thou forget the things which thine eyes have seen, and lest they depart from thy heart all the days of thy life: but teach them thy sons, and thy sons' sons;"

17.	Question:	Recap the words of Moses from verse 5.
	Answer:	
18.	Question:	What does verse 6 say they were to do?
	Answer:	
19.	Question:	Why should they do this? (vs 6)
	Answer:	
20.	Question:	What would other nations say about them? (vs 6)
	Answer:	
21.	Question:	What is the question asked in verse 7?
	Answer:	

SECTION 1 — WATCHING. WAITING. WARNING. — Unarmed & Ill-Equipped

22.	Question:	What does verse 9 say to them and why?
	Answer:	
23.	Question:	Do you think verse 9 is an important verse? Explain your reasoning?
	Answer:	
24.	Question:	From what you know of the Bible, did the children of Israel obey this Word from God?
	Answer:	

1 Samuel 13:13 And Samuel said to Saul, a) Thou hast done foolishly: b) thou hast not **kept** <8104> the commandment of YeHoVaH thy God, which he commanded thee: c) for now would YeHoVaH have established thy kingdom upon Israel for ever.		
25.	Comment:	The prophet Samuel is speaking to King Saul, early on in Saul's time as king.
	Question:	What does Samuel say to Saul in verse 13 a)?
	Answer:	
26.	Question:	What does Samuel say to Saul in verse 13 b)?
	Answer:	

Chapter 1 Unarmed?

27.	Question:	What happened as a result of Saul's choices? (vs 13 c)
	Answer:	

Psalm 37:34 Wait on YeHoVaH, and **keep <8104>** his way, and he shall exalt thee to inherit the land: when the wicked are cut off, thou shalt see it.		
28.	Question:	What is required, under the First Covenant, to inherit the land? (2 things)
	Answer:		
29.	Question:	After doing 2 things, what does the Lord do? (2 things)
	Answer:		

Proverbs 10:17 He is in the way of life that **keepeth <8104>** instruction *(correction)*: but he that refuseth reproof erreth.		
30.	Question:	What happens to the one that keeps instruction?
	Answer:	
31.	Question:	What happens to the one that refuses reproof?
	Answer:	

32. Using a Strong's Concordance, or an online Bible resource, look up the HEBREW word # 8104. Fill in the blanks below. *(The Hebrew is already typed in the box for you, as well as how KJV interpreted it!)*

Hebrew Word #8104 שמר	Meaning:
Pronounced:	
A primitive root, verb	
KJV interpreted as keep 283, observe 46, heed 35, keeper 28, preserve 21, beware 9, mark 8, watchman 8, wait 7, watch 7, regard 5, save 2, misc. 9; 468 times used	

33. We are now going to look back on these questions # 1 to 31 and look at those brackets with the numbers about which we spoke earlier. First, select a coloured highlighter, pencil crayon or crayon. Second, go back over each of the scriptures found in questions # 1 to 31. Find the bracketed number (e.g. <8104>). In front of that number, you'll find a bolded word. Highlight each word before the bracketed number <8104>[13].

---

[13] # 8104 is a reference number to a Hebrew Word found in a reference source known as Strong's Concordance

Chapter 1 — Unarmed?

34. KJV translated the Hebrew word שמר as "keep" (keepeth/kept) or "heed". In the space below, recap what one is to "keep", and what one is to "heed".

Keep/Keepeth/kept	Heed

Read the following scripture and answer the questions.

Genesis 3: 23 "Therefore YeHoVaH God sent him forth from the garden of Eden, to till <05647>the ground from whence he was taken."		
35.	Question:	Verse 23 tells us what Adam and Eve were to do when they left the garden. What is it that they were to do?
	Answer:	(continue your answer here)

45

36. Using a Strong's Concordance, or an online Bible resource, look up the HEBREW word # 5647. (Please note, some resources require the number 0 inserted before doing a search, e.g. 05647.) After finding the Hebrew word and its meaning, fill in the blanks below. Please note, we have already written the Hebrew word in for you.

Hebrew Word #5647 עבד	Meaning:
Pronounced:	
A primitive root, verb	
KJV interpreted as serve 227, do 15, till 9, servant 5, work 5, worshippers 5, service 4, dress 2, labour 2, ear 2, misc 14; 290	

37. There are 3 basic Hebrew Letters that make up this word. If you know the names of these letters, please write them in the appropriate space. You'll find a reference chart in the Appendix which lists the Hebrew alphabet.

Hebrew Letter	Name of Letter
ע	
ב	
ד	

Turn to your Bibles to the book of Nehemiah. Read the Chapters 1 to 4. Then, in the provided spaces, write a short recap **(the main thoughts)** of each chapter.

38.   Nehemiah Chapter 1

SECTION 1 — WATCHING. WAITING. WARNING. — Unarmed & Ill-Equipped

39. Nehemiah Chapter 2

40. Nehemiah Chapter 3

41. Nehemiah Chapter 4

Chapter 1 — Unarmed?

PRECIOUS MOMENTS RECAP

42.	QUESTION:	Review this workbook chapter. Pick out the scriptures that spoke to you the most. Write at least one of those scriptures in the space below.
	ANSWER:	
43.	QUESTION:	What specific truth from the scriptures you studied in this workbook chapter speaks to you. Write that truth in the space below.
	ANSWER:	

SECTION 1   WATCHING. WAITING. WARNING.   Unarmed & Ill-Equipped

		(continue your answer here)
44.	QUESTION:	Think of how you can apply this scripture to your life. Enter those thoughts in the space below.
	ANSWER:	

CHAPTER 2 – Why Armed?

Don't forget to precede this chapter with prayer and an invitation to the Holy Spirit to help you. "Open thou mine eyes, that I may behold wondrous things out of thy law"[14] is always a good way to begin your prayer!

Read the following scripture and answer the questions:

John 10:"1 ¶ Verily, verily, I say unto you, He that entereth not by the door into the sheepfold, but climbeth up some other way, the same is a thief and a robber. 2 But he that entereth in by the door is the shepherd of the sheep. 3 To him the porter openeth; and the sheep hear his voice: and he calleth his own sheep by name, and leadeth them out. 4 And when he putteth forth his own sheep, he goeth before them, and the sheep follow him: for they know his voice. 5 And a stranger will they not follow, but will flee from him: for they know not the voice of strangers. 6 This parable spake Jesus unto them: but they understood not what things they were which he spake unto them.		
1.	Comment:	Yeshua is speaking to His disciples. Verses 1 to 5 record the parable He taught.

---

[14] Psalm 119:18

SECTION 1

WATCHING. WAITING. WARNING.

Unarmed & Ill-Equipped

2.	Question:	Recap the parable in verses 1 to 6.
	Answer:	

John 10: 7 Then said Jesus unto them again, Verily, verily, I say unto you, I am the door of the sheep. 8 All that ever came before me are thieves and robbers: but the sheep did not hear them. 9 I am the door: by me if any man enter in, he shall be saved, and shall go in and out, and find pasture. 10 The thief cometh not, but for to steal, and to kill, and to destroy: I am come that they might have life, and that they might have [it] more abundantly."

3.	Question:	Who is the door according to verse 7?
	Answer:	
4.	Question:	Who were they that came before Him? (vs 8)
	Answer:	
5.	Question:	How did the sheep respond? (vs 8)
	Answer:	

6.	Question:	What happens to the person who enters in through Yeshua? (vs 9)
	Answer:	

7.	Question:	Why does the thief come?
	Answer:	

8.	Question:	Why did Yeshua come?
	Answer:	

Genesis 4: 3 ¶ And in process of time it came to pass, that Cain brought of the fruit of the ground an offering unto YeHoVaH. 4 And Abel, he also brought of the firstlings of his flock and of the fat thereof. And YeHoVaH had respect unto Abel and to his offering: 5 But unto Cain and to his offering he had not respect. And Cain was very wroth, and his countenance fell. 6 ¶ And YeHoVaH said unto Cain, Why art thou wroth? and why is thy countenance fallen? 7 If thou doest well, shalt thou not be accepted? and if thou doest not well, sin lieth at the door. And unto thee shall be his desire, and thou shalt rule over him.

9.	Question:	What kind of an offering did Cain bring the Lord? (vs 3)
	Answer:	

10.	Question:	What kind of an offering did Abel bring to the Lord? (vs 4)
	Answer:	

11.	Question:	How did the Lord receive the offering from Abel? (vs 4)
	Answer:	
12.	Question:	How did the Lord look at Cain's offering? (vs 5)
	Answer:	
13.	Question:	How did Cain respond to God attitude? (vs 5)
	Answer:	
14.	Question:	How did God respond to Cain's attitude? (vs 6)
	Answer:	
15.	Question:	What does God tell Cain in verse 7?
	Answer:	
16.	Question:	Do you know why God did not respect the offering of Cain. Explain your answer.
	Answer:	

17. God received a sin offering from Abel. Look up in the Bible, or online, what constitutes *a sin offering* and when it should be brought before the Lord. Write a recap of a sin offering in the space provided on the next page.

(your answer here)

18. Cain brought God *a grain offering*. Look up in your Bible, or online, what constitutes a grain offering, and when it should be brought before the Lord. Write a recap of a grain offering in the space below.

SECTION 1

Luke 13:31 ¶ The same day there came certain of the Pharisees, saying unto him, Get thee out, and depart hence: for Herod will kill thee. 32 And he said unto them, Go ye, and tell that fox, Behold, I cast out devils, and I do cures to day and to morrow, and the third day I shall be perfected. 33 Nevertheless I must walk to day, and to morrow, and the day following: for it cannot be that a prophet perish out of Jerusalem. 34 O Jerusalem, Jerusalem, which killest the prophets, and stonest them that are sent unto thee; how often would I have gathered thy children together, as a hen doth gather her brood under her wings, and ye would not! 35 Behold, your house is left unto you desolate: and verily I say unto you, Ye shall not see me, until the time come when ye shall say, Blessed is he that cometh in the name of the Lord.

19.	Question:	What did the Pharisees say to Yeshua in verse 31?
	Answer:	
20.	Question:	Why do think the Pharisees would say that to Yeshua?
	Answer:	
21.	Question:	How did Yeshua respond to the Pharisees? (vs 32-33)
	Answer:	
22.	Question:	What did Yeshua say about Jerusalem? (vs 34)
	Answer:	

		(continue your answer here)
23.	Question:	What did Yeshua prophesy in verse 35?
	Answer:	
24.	Question:	How do you think Yeshua declared this message? (e.g. with weeping, tears, joy, etc.) Explain your viewpoint[15].
	Answer:	
25.	Question:	Jerusalem has risen as a city once again! As you look at Jerusalem through the news media, or explore Israel online or in person, do you think Yeshua would weep over Jerusalem *as it is today?* *(Don't forget to explain your reasoning)*

---

[15] Whenever you are asked for a viewpoint, support your answer with scripture wherever you can.

SECTION 1
WATCHING. WAITING. WARNING.
Unarmed & Ill-Equipped

	Answer:	

Zechariah 1:1 ¶ In the eighth month, in the second year of Darius, came the word of YeHoVaH unto Zechariah, the son of Berechiah, the son of Iddo the prophet, saying, 2 The LORD hath been sore displeased with your fathers. 3 Therefore say thou unto them, Thus saith YeHoVaH of hosts; Turn <7725> ye unto me, saith YeHoVaH of hosts, and I will turn <7725> unto you, saith YeHoVaH of hosts.

26.	Question:	There are certain elements of time given to us in this verse in order to know the timeframe of Israel. In the provided space, write out the 2 phrases referring to time.
	Answer:	i
		ii
27.	Question:	From these elements of time, do you know the setting when these words came? Write out your answers below. (If you don't know and you wish to use a commentary, feel free to do so.)
	Answer:	
		(continue your answer here)

28.	Question:	What information does verse 2 tell us?
	Answer:	
29.	Question:	In verse 3, the word "therefore" appears. Write down what it is there for![16]
	Answer:	
30.	Question:	What does the Lord say in verse 3?
	Answer:	

---

[16] Always a good idea to ask that, whenever you see a "wherefore" or "therefore".

31.	Question:	How many times does it say, "saith the Lord" in verse 3?
	Answer:	
32.	Question:	Do you think there is anything significant in repeating "saith the Lord"? Explain your reasoning.
	Answer:	

33. Using a Strong's Concordance or online source, look up the HEBREW WORD # 7725. Fill in the blanks on the next page. *(Don't worry about writing the Hebrew letters as we have already typed them in for you!)*

Hebrew Word #7725 שׁוּב	Meaning:
Pronounced:	
A primitive root, verb	
KJV interpreted return 391, again 248, turn 123, back 65, away 56, restore 39, bring 34, render 19, answer 18, recompense 8, recover 6, deliver 5, put 5, withdraw 5, requite 4, misc 40; 1066	

34. There are 3 basic Hebrew Letters that make up this word. If you know the names of these letters, please write them in the appropriate space below. You'll find a reference chart in the Appendix which lists the Hebrew alphabet.

Hebrew Letter	Name of Letter
שׁ	
וּ	
ב	

Before ending this Chapter, let's take a quick look at what the Apostolic writings say regarding a believer's defence system. It is a passage, which I trust, you know well! If not, please consider reading it several times.

SECTION 1   Unarmed & Ill-Equipped

Ephesians 6:11 Put on the whole armour of God, that ye may be able to stand against the wiles of the devil. 12 a) For we wrestle not against flesh and blood, b) but against principalities, against powers, against the rulers of the darkness of this world, against spiritual wickedness in high [places].		
35.	Question:	What does this scripture say regarding "armour"? (vs 11)
	Answer:	
36.	Question:	Why does verse 11 say we should wear it?
	Answer:	
37.	Question:	Why does verse 12 a) say we should wear it?
	Answer:	
38.	Question:	Why does verse 12 b) say we should wear it?
	Answer:	

Chapter 2 — Why Armed?

39. Using a Strong's Concordance or online source, look up the GREEK WORD # 3180. Fill in the blanks below.

Greek Word #3180 μεθοδεία	Meaning
Pronounced:	
A primitive root, verb	
KJV interprets this word as lie in wait 1, wile 1; 2	

Ephesians 6: 13 Wherefore take unto you the whole armour of God, that ye may be able to withstand in the evil day, and having done all, to stand.		
40.	Question:	Verse 13 begins with "wherefore". To what does it refer?
	Answer:	
41.	Question:	What is one to do, according to verse 13?
	Answer:	
42.	Question:	Why is one to do this? (2 reasons)
	Answer:	i
		ii

SECTION 1

WATCHING. WAITING. WARNING.

Unarmed & Ill-Equipped

Ephesians 6:14 Stand therefore, having your loins girt about with truth, and having on the breastplate of righteousness; 15 And your feet shod with the preparation of the gospel of peace; 16 Above all, taking the shield of faith, wherewith ye shall be able to quench all the fiery darts of the wicked. 17 And take the helmet of salvation, and the sword of the Spirit, which is the word of God: 18 Praying always with all prayer and supplication in the Spirit, and watching thereunto with all perseverance and supplication for all saints;		
43.	Question:	To what does the "therefore" refer in verse 14?
	Answer:	
44.	Comment:	Pieces of armour are described in verse 14 to 17.[17]
	Question:	List the pieces of armour in verse 14. (2 pcs)
	Answer:	
45.	Question:	List the piece of armour in verse 15.
	Answer:	
46.	Question:	What piece is mentioned in verse 16?

---

[17] Paul used this armour metaphorically. Here, simply describe the armour. Later, there'll be information on its meaning in the Christian life.

	Answer:	
47.	Question:	List the pieces of armour in verse 17. (2 pcs)
	Answer:	
48.	Question:	What does verse 18 advise?
	Answer:	

49. Using a Strong's Concordance or online source, look up the GREEK WORD # 69. Fill in the blanks in the provided space.

Greek Word #69	Meaning:
ἀγρυπνέω	
Pronounced:	
A primitive root, verb	

SECTION 1 — WATCHING. WAITING. WARNING. — Unarmed & Ill-Equipped

50. Why do you think that Paul, the apostle, in his letter to the Ephesians, thought it necessary to add the word "watch" to the believer's armour?

51. At this point, you might not know exactly what "watching" is all about, or how to do it. Nevertheless, write a few comments in the space below as to what you think "watching" is about, and if you know "what the believer" is to watch, record that information as well.

Chapter 2 — Why Armed?

52. If you are feeling a little creative, and up to having a little fun, consider drawing a picture of yourself wearing your armour. If you like to use stick figures, that is really OK!

PRECIOUS MOMENTS RECAP

53.	QUESTION:	Review this workbook chapter. Pick out the scriptures that spoke to you the most. Write at least one of those scriptures in the space below.
	ANSWER:	

SECTION 1

WATCHING. WAITING. WARNING.

Unarmed & Ill-Equipped

54.	QUESTION:	What specific truth from the scriptures you studied in this workbook chapter speaks to you. Write that truth in the space below.
	ANSWER:	
55.	QUESTION:	Think of how you can apply this scripture to your life. Enter those thoughts in the space below.
	ANSWER:	

CHAPTER 3 – Why Change?

Just another reminder to begin this workbook section with prayer and an invitation to the Holy Spirit to help you. After prayer, read the following scripture and answer the questions.

John 14: 28 Ye have heard how I said unto you, I go away, and come again unto you. If ye loved me, ye would rejoice, because I said, I go unto the Father: for my Father is greater than I. 29 And now I have told you before it come to pass, that, when it is come to pass, ye might believe. 30 Hereafter I will not talk much with you: for the prince of this cometh, and hath nothing in me.		
1.	Question:	Recap the things Yeshua said to His Disciples in these verses, paying special attention to verse 30.
	Answer:	

SECTION 1　　WATCHING. WAITING. WARNING.　　Unarmed & Ill-Equipped

> 1 Peter 4:1 Forasmuch then as Christ hath suffered for us in the flesh, arm yourselves likewise with the same mind: for he that hath suffered in the flesh hath ceased from sin; 2 That he no longer should live the rest of his time in the flesh to the lusts of men, but to the will of God. 3 For the time past of our life may suffice us to have wrought the will of the Gentiles, when we walked in lasciviousness, lusts, excess of wine, revellings, banquetings, and abominable idolatries: 4 ¶ Wherein they think it strange that ye run not with them to the same excess of riot, speaking evil of you: 5 Who shall give account to him that is ready to judge the quick and the dead. 6 For for this cause was the gospel preached also to them that are dead, that they might be judged according to men in the flesh, but live according to God in the spirit. 7 ¶ But the end of all things is at hand: be ye therefore sober, and watch unto prayer.

2.	Question:	Recap the message of Peter in these verses. [18]
	Answer:	
3.	Question:	In verse 7 it says, "be sober and watch unto prayer." Using a Strong's Concordance or online source, refer to the meaning of the Greek words for "sober" and "watch". Then recap what you believe the Apostle Peter means by the words "be sober and watch".

---

[18] If you are not familiar with this scripture (or any other scripture at any time in this workbook) be sure and check surrounding passages of scripture.

	Answer:	

4. Using a Strong's Concordance or online source, look up the GREEK WORD # 3695. Fill in the blanks below.

Greek Word #3695	Meaning:
ὁπλίζω	
Pronounced:	
KJV interprets this word as arm (one's) self with 1;	

SECTION 1 — WATCHING. WAITING. WARNING. — Unarmed & Ill-Equipped

1 Peter 5: 8 Be sober, be vigilant; because your adversary the devil, as a roaring lion, walketh about, seeking whom he may devour;"		
5.	Question:	What specific things does Peter advise the believer in this verse?
	Answer:	
6.	Question:	Why does Peter advise this?
	Answer:	
7.	Question:	Put this verse in your own words.
	Answer:	

John 14: 10 Believest thou not that I am in the Father, and the Father in me? the words that I speak unto you I speak not of myself: but the Father that dwelleth in me, he doeth the works.		
8.	Question:	Recap Yeshua's message.
	Answer:	

***1 Kings 3: 7 And now, O LORD my God, thou hast made thy servant king instead of David my father: and I am but a little child: I know not how to go out or come in. 8 And thy servant is in the midst of thy people which thou hast chosen, a great people, that cannot be numbered nor counted for multitude. 9 Give therefore thy servant an understanding heart to judge thy people, that I may discern between good and bad: for who is able to judge this thy so great a people? 10 And the speech pleased the Lord, that Solomon had asked this thing. 11 And God said unto him, Because thou hast asked this thing, and hast not asked for thyself long life; neither hast asked riches for thyself, nor hast asked the life of thine enemies; but hast asked for thyself understanding to discern judgment; 12 Behold, I have done according to thy words: lo, I have given thee a wise and an understanding heart; so that there was none like thee before thee, neither after thee shall any arise like unto thee. 13 And I have also given thee that which thou hast not asked, both riches, and honour: so that there shall not be any among the kings like unto thee all thy days. 14 And if thou wilt walk in my ways, to **keep <8104>** my statutes and my commandments, as thy father David did walk, then I will lengthen thy days.			

9.	Comment:	In the above scripture, the Lord spoke to Solomon at the beginning of his reign as King.
	Question:	List below what God gave Solomon.
	Answer:	
10.	Question:	In verse 14, we hear of a conditional promise given to Solomon. Write out the conditional promise.
	Answer:	

11. Using a Strong's Concordance or online source, look up the HEBREW WORD # 8104. Fill in the blanks below.

Hebrew Word 8104 שמר	Meaning:
Pronounced:	
a primitive root; verb	
KJV interprets this word keep 283, observe 46, heed 35, keeper 28, preserve 21, beware 9, mark 8, watchman 8, wait 7, watch 7, regard 5, save 2, misc 9; 468	
Repeat of 1 Kings 3:14	

14 And if thou wilt walk in my ways, to **keep <8104>** my statutes and my commandments, as thy father David did walk, then I will lengthen thy days.		
12.	Question:	Taking the interpretation of the Hebrew word שמר Strong's # 8104, write out, in your own words, what God asked of Solomon.
	Answer:	

***1 Kings 11:1 ¶ But king Solomon loved many strange women, together with the daughter of Pharaoh, women of the Moabites, Ammonites, Edomites, Zidonians, and Hittites; 2 Of the nations concerning which YeHoVaH said unto the children of Israel, Ye shall not go in to them, neither shall they come in unto you: for surely they will turn away your heart after their gods: Solomon clave unto these in love. 3 And he had seven hundred wives, princesses, and three hundred concubines: and his wives turned away his heart. 4 For it came to pass, when Solomon was old, that his wives turned away his heart after other gods: and his heart was not perfect with YeHoVaH his God, as was the heart of David his father. 5 For Solomon went after Ashtoreth the goddess of the Zidonians, and after Milcom the abomination of the Ammonites. 6 And Solomon did evil in the sight of YeHoVaH, and went not fully after YeHoVaH, as did David his father. 7 Then did Solomon build an high place for Chemosh, the abomination of Moab, in the hill that is before Jerusalem, and for Molech, the abomination of the children of Ammon. 8 And likewise did he for all his strange wives, which burnt incense and sacrificed unto their gods. 9 ¶ And YeHoVaH was angry with Solomon, because his heart was turned from YeHoVaH God of Israel, which had appeared unto him twice, 10 And had commanded him concerning this thing, that he should not go after other gods: but he

SECTION 1

WATCHING. WAITING. WARNING.

Unarmed & Ill-Equipped

kept not that which YeHoVaH commanded. 11 Wherefore YeHoVaH said unto Solomon, Forasmuch as this is done of thee, and thou hast not kept my covenant and my statutes, which I have commanded thee, I will surely rend the kingdom from thee, and will give it to thy servant. 12 Notwithstanding in thy days I will not do it for David thy father's sake: but I will rend it out of the hand of thy son. 13 Howbeit I will not rend away all the kingdom; but will give one tribe to thy son for David my servant's sake, and for Jerusalem's sake which I have chosen. 14 ¶ And YeHoVaH stirred up an adversary unto Solomon, Hadad the Edomite: he was of the king's seed in Edom.

13.	Question:	After reading this passage, go back to the previous scripture in question # 12, 1 Kings 3:14. Did Solomon do what the Lord required? Give reasons for your answers.
	Answer:	

14.	Question:	What do you think was the bottom line of Solomon's behaviour?
	Answer:	

Remaining in the book of Kings, we are going to quickly look at another man to whom the Lord made promises. That man is Jeroboam. As you read the scripture below, you will see Strong's # 8104 bolded. Remember what you learned about that word!

> ***1 Kings 11:31 And he said to Jeroboam, Take thee ten pieces: for thus saith YeHoVaH, the God of Israel, Behold, I will rend the kingdom out of the hand of Solomon, and will give ten tribes to thee: 32 (But he shall have one tribe for my servant David's sake, and for Jerusalem's sake, the city which I have chosen out of all the tribes of Israel:) 33 Because that they have forsaken me, and have worshipped Ashtoreth the goddess of the Zidonians, Chemosh the god of the Moabites, and Milcom the god of the children of Ammon, and have not walked in my ways, to do [that which is] right in mine eyes, and [to keep[19]] my statutes and my

---

[19] This is not # 8104 but is a word interjected here by KJV which is not included in the original text.

SECTION 1
WATCHING. WAITING. WARNING.
Unarmed & Ill-Equipped

> judgments, as [did] David his father. 34 Howbeit I will not take the whole kingdom out of his hand: but I will make him prince all the days of his life for David my servant's sake, whom I chose, because he **kept <8104>** my commandments and my statutes: 35 But I will take the kingdom out of his son's hand, and will give it unto thee, [even] ten tribes. 36 And unto his son will I give one tribe, that David my servant may have a light alway before me in Jerusalem, the city which I have chosen me to put my name there. 37 And I will take thee, and thou shalt reign according to all that thy soul desireth, and shalt be king over Israel. 38 And it shall be, if thou wilt hearken unto all that I command thee, and wilt walk in my ways, and do [that is] right in my sight, to **keep <8104>** my statutes and my commandments, as David my servant did; that I will be with thee, and build thee a sure house, as I built for David, and will give Israel unto thee.

15.	Question:	What did God promise Jeroboam?
	Answer:	
16.	Question:	What was the condition?
	Answer:	

***1 Kings 14:7 ¶ Go, tell Jeroboam, Thus saith YeHoVaH God of Israel, Forasmuch as I exalted thee from among the people, and made thee prince over my people Israel, 8 And rent the kingdom away from the house of David, and gave it thee: and [yet] thou hast not been as my servant David, who kept <8104> my commandments, and who followed me with all his heart, to do [that] only [which was] right in mine eyes; 9 But hast done evil above all that were before thee: for thou hast gone and made thee other gods, and molten images, to provoke me to anger, and hast cast me behind thy back: 10 Therefore, behold, I will bring evil upon the house of Jeroboam, and will cut off from Jeroboam him that pisseth against the wall, [and] him that is shut up and left in Israel, and will take away the remnant of the house of Jeroboam, as a man taketh away dung, till it be all gone."

17.	Question:	Recap what these scriptures say about Jeroboam.
	Answer:	
18.	Question:	What would God do to Jeroboam?
	Answer:	

SECTION 1

WATCHING. WAITING. WARNING.

Unarmed & Ill-Equipped

19.	Question:	What do these scriptures say about King David?
	Answer:	

Chapter 3   Why Change?

20. Go back over the scriptures marked with 3 stars: ***. As you re-read them, take note of the 3 kings mentioned, *(David, Solomon, and Jeroboam)*, and the promises God made to them. All three kings were asked to keep <8104> God's commandments, laws and statutes but only King David managed to do so. In the space below, write out why you think the other two kings could not keep their part of the covenant with the Lord?

Acts 13:22 And when he had removed him, he raised up unto them David to be their king; to whom also he gave testimony, and said, I have found David the son of Jesse, a man after mine own heart, which shall fulfil all my will.		
21.	Question:	What was said about King David?
	Answer:	

SECTION 1

22.	Question:	Why do you think David could keep his part of the covenant with God?
	Answer:	
23.	Question:	Do you think the covenant, in which you are part, through Yeshua, requires the same commitment as that of Solomon, David and Jeroboam? Explain your reasoning.
	Answer:	
24.	Question:	Looking at all 3 Kings studied in this Chapter, what can we learn from them?
	Answer:	Solomon

		Jeroboam	
		David	
25.	Question:	Do you think a believer can fail in their covenant commitment to God? Explain your answer.	
	Answer:		

SECTION 1 *WATCHING. WAITING. WARNING.* Unarmed & Ill-Equipped

> James 1:14 But every man is tempted, when he is drawn away of his own lust, and enticed. 15 Then when lust hath conceived, it bringeth forth sin: and sin, when it is finished, bringeth forth death."

26.	Question:	According to verse 14, how is a person tempted?
	Answer:	
27.	Question:	What happens to "lust" once it has conceived? (vs 15)
	Answer:	
28.	Question:	What is the end of sin? (vs 15)
	Answer:	

Chapter 3 — Why Change?

> Mark 14: 31But he spake the more vehemently, If I should die with thee, I will not deny thee in any wise. Likewise also said they all. 32 ¶ And they came to a place which was named Gethsemane: and he saith to his disciples, Sit ye here, while I shall pray. 33 And he taketh with him Peter and James and John, and began to be sore amazed, and to be very heavy; 34 And saith unto them, My soul is exceeding sorrowful unto death: tarry ye here, and watch. 35 And he went forward a little, and fell on the ground, and prayed that, if it were possible, the hour might pass from him. 36 And he said, Abba, Father, all things [are] possible unto thee; take away this cup from me: nevertheless not what I will, but what thou wilt. 37 And he cometh, and findeth them sleeping, and saith unto Peter, Simon, sleepest thou? couldest not thou watch one hour? 38 Watch ye and pray, lest ye enter into temptation. The spirit truly [is] ready, but the flesh [is] weak."

29.	Comment:	Earlier, Yeshua told Peter that he would deny Him. Peter insisted that would not happen as he would die with Yeshua. Then they went to the Garden of Gethsemane.
30.	Question:	Recap the words of Peter and the disciples from verse 31.
	Answer:	
31.	Question:	What did Yeshua say in verse 32?
	Answer:	
32.	Question:	Who did Yeshua take with Him? (vs 33)
	Answer:	

SECTION 1 — WATCHING. WAITING. WARNING. — Unarmed & Ill-Equipped

33.	Question:	What did Yeshua say to them in verse 34? (3 things)
	Answer:	

34.	Question:	Recap verses 35 to 36.
	Answer:	

35.	Question:	When Yeshua returned to His disciples what did He find? (vs 37)
	Answer:	

36.	Question:	What question did Yeshua asked them according to verse 37?
	Answer:	

37.	Question:	What did Yeshua say in verse 38?
	Answer:	

Chapter 3 — Why Change?

Luke 21: 7 And they asked him, saying, Master, but when shall these things be? and what sign will there be when these things shall come to pass?	*Luke 21:36 "Watch ye therefore, and pray always, that ye may be accounted worthy to escape all these things that shall come to pass, and to stand before the Son of man."*
38. Instruction	Before answering the question, in your Bible read Luke 31:5-6.
Question:	In Luke 21:7 the disciples asked Yeshua a question. What was the question?
Answer:	

Turn to your Bibles. Read Luke 21:8 to 36 where Yeshua explains much to His disciples in order to answer their question. Your aim here, is to familiarize yourself with the text. Then move on to the next question.

39. Question:	Re-Read verse 36 and then write below what 2 things Yeshua told the disciples to do.
Answer:	
40. Question:	What reasons does Yeshua give them, in verse 36, as to why they should do these things?
Answer:	

In the following Scriptures, the word שמר Strong's # 8104 is used. Read the scripture remembering the meaning of the word #8104. Write an expanded meaning of the verse in the space below the verse.		
41.	Scripture:	Genesis 28: 15 And, behold, I [am] with thee, and will **keep <8104>** thee in all [places] whither thou goest, and will bring thee again into this land; for I will not leave thee, until I have done [that] which I have spoken to thee of."
	Answer:	
42.	Scripture:	Numbers 6:24 The LORD bless thee, and **keep <8104>** thee:"
	Answer:	
43.	Scripture:	Jeremiah 51:12 Then said YeHoVaH unto me, Thou hast well seen: for I will hasten my word to perform it."

	Answer:	

44. Read the following scriptures and in the space below the text write out what they say about the Lord.

Psalm 47:8 God reigneth over the heathen: God sitteth upon the throne of his holiness.

Psalm 45:6 "Thy throne, O God, [is] for ever and ever: the sceptre of thy kingdom [is] a right sceptre.

SECTION 1

WATCHING. WAITING. WARNING.

Unarmed & Ill-Equipped

> 2 Chronicles 16:9 For the eyes of YeHoVaH run to and fro throughout the whole earth, to shew himself strong in the behalf of [them] whose heart [is] perfect toward him. Herein thou hast done foolishly: therefore from henceforth thou shalt have wars."

> Zechariah 4:10 For who hath despised the day of small things? for they shall rejoice, and shall see the plummet in the hand of Zerubbabel [with] those seven; they [are] the eyes of YeHoVaH, which run to and fro through the whole earth."

> 2 Timothy 2: 3 Thou therefore endure hardness, as a good soldier of Jesus Christ. 4 No man that warreth entangleth himself with the affairs of [this] life; that he may please him who hath chosen him to be a soldier. 5 And if a man also strive for masteries, [yet] is he not crowned, except he strive lawfully. 6 The husbandman that laboureth must be first partaker of the fruits. 7 Consider what I say; and the Lord give thee understanding in all things."

45.	Question:	What does verse 3 tell us to do?
	Answer:	

		(continue your answer here)
46.	Question:	According to verse 4, what does a good solder avoid and why?
	Answer:	
47.	Question:	According to verse 5, why is one crowned?
	Answer:	
48.	Question:	What does verse 6 say about the husbandman?
	Answer:	
49.	Question:	What does verse 7 ask of the Lord?

SECTION 1   WATCHING. WAITING. WARNING.   Unarmed & Ill-Equipped

	Answer:	
50.	Question:	Re-read these verses. Recap the overall meaning in the space below.
	Answer:	

51. After reading the scriptures in this Chapter, what do you think about a believer living and responding like a soldier? Write out your thoughts below and on the next page.

PRECIOUS MOMENTS RECAP

52.	QUESTION:	Review this workbook chapter. Pick out the scriptures that spoke to you the most. Write at least one of those scriptures in the space below.
	ANSWER:	
53.	QUESTION:	What specific truth from the scriptures you studied in this workbook chapter speaks to you. Write that truth in the space below.
	ANSWER:	(continue your answer here)

SECTION 1 — WATCHING. WAITING. WARNING. — Unarmed & Ill-Equipped

54.	QUESTION:	Think of how you can apply this scripture to your life. Enter those thoughts in the space below.
	ANSWER:	

COURSE 403 continued
WATCHING. WAITING. WARNING.

SECTION 2 –

Armed & Ready

WATCHING

CHAPTER 4 – Targeted Recruitment

Don't forget to preface this Chapter with prayer!
***

As we begin this Chapter, we will start by looking up a Greek Word, and referencing some scriptures which contain that word.

1. Look up the Greek Word (Strong's # 1127) and fill in the blanks in the space below.

Greek Word # 1127 ρηγορεύω Rooted from # 1453	Meaning:
Pronounced:	
A verb	
KJV interprets this word as watch 21, wake 1, be vigilant 1; 23	

WATCHING. WAITING. WARNING.

SECTION 2　　　　　　　　　　　　　　　　　　Armed & Ready

Root Greek Word	
Greek Word # 1453 ἐγείρω	Meaning:
Pronounced:	
A verb	
KJV interprets this word as rise 36, raise 28, arise 27, raise up 23, rise up 8, rise again 5, raise again 4, misc. 10; 1414	

2. There are 23 scriptures written on the next pages. Each scripture uses a word (# **1127** in Strong's Concordance). Your job is to select 5 scriptures. Record them in their proper provided space, and then go to your Bible and read some surrounding text! After that, recap the meaning of the verse containing the word interpreted by KJV.

SCRIPTURES FOR QUESTION # 2:

i. Matthew 24:42 Watch <1127> therefore: for ye know not what hour your Lord doth come.

ii. Matthew 24:43 But know this, that if the goodman of the house had known in what watch the thief would come, he would have watched <1127>, and would not have suffered his house to be broken up.

iii. Matthew 25:13 Watch <1127> therefore, for ye know neither the day nor the hour wherein the Son of man cometh.

iv. Matthew 26:38 Then saith he unto them, My soul is exceeding sorrowful, even unto death: tarry ye here, and watch <1127> with me.

v. Matthew 26:40 And he cometh unto the disciples, and findeth them asleep, and saith unto Peter, What, could ye not watch <1127> with me one hour?
vi. Matthew 26:41 Watch <1127> and pray, that ye enter not into temptation: the spirit indeed is willing, but the flesh is weak.
vii. Mark 13:34 For the Son of man is as a man taking a far journey, who left his house, and gave authority to his servants, and to every man his work, and commanded the porter to watch <1127>.
viii. Mark 13:35 Watch ye <1127> therefore: for ye know not when the master of the house cometh, at even, or at midnight, or at the cockcrowing, or in the morning:
ix. Mark 13:37 And what I say unto you I say unto all, Watch <1127>.
x. Mark 14:34 And saith unto them, My soul is exceeding sorrowful unto death: tarry ye here, and watch <1127>.
xi. Mark 14:37 And he cometh, and findeth them sleeping, and saith unto Peter, Simon, sleepest thou? couldest not thou watch <1127> one hour?
xii. Mark 14:38 Watch ye <1127> and pray, lest ye enter into temptation. The spirit truly is ready, but the flesh is weak.
xiii. Luke 12:37 Blessed are those servants, whom the lord when he cometh shall find watching <1127>: verily I say unto you, that he shall gird himself, and make them to sit down to meat, and will come forth and serve them.
xiv. Luke 12:39 And this know, that if the goodman of the house had known what hour the thief would come, he would have watched <1127>, and not have suffered his house to be broken through.
xv. Acts 20:31 Therefore watch <1127>, and remember, that by the space of three years I ceased not to warn every one night and day with tears.
xvi. 1 Corinthians 16:13 Watch ye <1127>, stand fast in the faith, quit you like men, be strong.

WATCHING. WAITING. WARNING.

SECTION 2   Armed & Ready

xvii. Colossians 4:2 Continue in prayer, and watch <1127> in the same with thanksgiving;

xviii. 1 Thessalonians 5:6 Therefore let us not sleep, as do others; but let us watch <1127> and be sober.

xix. 1 Thessalonians 5:10 Who died for us, that, whether we wake <1127> or sleep, we should live together with him.

xx. 1 Peter 5:8 Be sober, be vigilant <1127>; because your adversary the devil, as a roaring lion, walketh about, seeking whom he may devour:

xxi. Revelation 3:2 Be watchful <1127>, and strengthen the things which remain, that are ready to die: for I have not found thy works perfect before God.

xxii. Revelation 3:3 Remember therefore how thou hast received and heard, and hold fast, and repent. If therefore thou shalt <1127> not watch <1127>, I will come on thee as a thief, and thou shalt not know what hour I will come upon thee.

xxiii. Revelation 16:15 Behold, I come as a thief. Blessed is he that watcheth <1127>, and keepeth his garments, lest he walk naked, and they see his shame.

Reference	Recap of verse content.
i.	
ii.	

iii.	
iv.	
v.	

3. Taking your textbook, review the former textbook chapters paying special attention to the mention of the idea of watching. Recap your findings in the appropriate space on the next pages.

WATCHING. WAITING. WARNING.

SECTION 2   Armed & Ready

a) Introduction	
b) Chapter One	
c) Chapter Two	

d) Chapter Three		4.

4. In the space below, write out what you have learned so far about watching.

5. Do you see any connection between watching and praying? If so, write out what you see using scripture references where possible.

WATCHING. WAITING. WARNING.
SECTION 2 — Armed & Ready

6. Write out a short paragraph describing the "watching" aspect of your life. Be honest with yourself and the Lord, here!

7. Looking at your spiritual life, would you say that you are unarmed and ill-equipped, or armed and ready, or some place in between? Explain why you think that way!

8. At the end of the third chapter, you read the following, *"Let's be those well trained, efficient soldiers who consistently obey Yeshua's command to watch and pray!*[20]*"*

    a) Where do you see your life fits in as a soldier for God's kingdom? Circle one of the following:

    >   no soldier   recruit   private

    >   corporal   sergeant   4 star general

    b) Do you think God wants you to go past where you are at present? Explain your reasoning!

    c) What will it take for you to cooperate with the Lord? (e.g. what will it cost you!)

---

[20] Matthew 26:41

WATCHING. WAITING. WARNING.

SECTION 2   Armed & Ready

9. **PERSONAL QUESTION NOT ASKED IN CLASS**[21]

    a) Are you willing to obey Yeshua's commands to watch and pray, even if it means you need to take a hard look at your life to see what must change in order to do that? (In your answer, write out what you think God might want you to do to change! This question is only between you and the Lord, so be as honest as you can with God!)

Read the following scriptures and answer the questions.

1 John 2:14 I have written unto you, fathers, because ye have known him [that is] from the beginning. I have written unto you, young men, because ye are strong, and the word of God abideth in you, and ye have overcome the wicked one. 15 Love not the world, neither the things [that are] in the world. If any man love the world, the love of the Father is not in him. 16 For all that [is] in the world, the lust of the flesh, and the lust of the eyes, and the pride of life, is not of the Father, but is of the world. 17 And the world passeth away, and the lust thereof: but he that doeth the will of God abideth for ever.		
10.	Question:	As you read this scripture, what is the main theme of it?

---

[21] At no time, whether in a seminar or a Bible Study group, do you even need to volunteer and answer! If you are called upon, and feel uncomfortable about sharing, simply say, "I'll pass on this one." Every study is intended to draw you closer to the Lord, never to embarrass you!

	Answer:	
11.	Question:	What abided in the young men? (vs 14)
	Answer:	
12.	Question:	Because of that which abided in the young men, what was possible? (vs 14)
	Answer:	
13.	Question:	What were these believers not to do? (vs 15)
	Answer:	
14.	Question:	If they did that thing, what did that say? (vs 15)
	Answer:	

WATCHING. WAITING. WARNING.

SECTION 2   Armed & Ready

15.	Question:	What does verse 16 say about the world?
	Answer:	
16.	Question:	Verse 17 says two things pass away. What are those two things?
	Answer:	
17.	Question:	Verse 17 speaks of something that abides forever. What is it?
	Answer:	
18.	Question:	What does this passage mean to you?
	Answer:	

John 15:1 ¶ I am the true vine, and my Father is the husbandman. 2 Every branch in me that beareth not fruit he taketh away: and every branch that beareth fruit, he purgeth it, that it may bring forth more fruit. 3 Now ye are clean through the word which I have spoken unto you. 4 Abide in me, and I in you. As the branch cannot bear fruit of itself, except it abide in the vine; no more can ye, except ye abide in me. 5 I am the vine, ye are the branches: He that abideth in me, and I in him, the same bringeth forth much fruit: for without me ye can do nothing. 6 If a man

abide not in me, he is cast forth as a branch, and is withered; and men gather them, and cast them into the fire, and they are burned. 7 If ye abide in me, and my words abide in you, ye shall ask what ye will, and it shall be done unto you. 8 Herein is my Father glorified, that ye bear much fruit; so shall ye be my disciples.

19.	Question:	What does Yeshua say about Himself and the Father in verse 1?
	Answer:	
20.	Question:	Put verse 2 into your own words.
	Answer:	
21.	Question:	What does verse 3 say regarding being clean?
	Answer:	
22.	Question:	Put verse 4 into your own words.
	Answer:	
23.	Question:	What does Yeshua say in verse 5?
	Answer:	
24.	Question:	What problem and solution is given to us in verse 6?
	Answer:	

SECTION 2 — WATCHING. WAITING. WARNING. — Armed & Ready

25.	Question:	Of what blessing does Yeshua speak in verse 7?
	Answer:	
26.	Question:	Recap verse 8 in your own words.
	Answer:	
27.	Question:	As you look at this scripture, do you see this "abiding" in your own life? If so, where, and if not, why not?
	Answer:	
28.	Question:	From your present knowledge of scripture, is this "abiding" about which Yeshua spoke, found anywhere in the Hebraic Scriptures? (First Covenant). If so, cite a few passages.
	Answer:	

29.	Question:	Using a Webster's dictionary or an online source, write the meaning of the word "abide" in the space below.
	Answer:	
30.	Question:	This section of the workbook is entitled, Armed and Ready. How do you think "abiding" fits in with the theme of being armed and ready?
	Answer:	

WATCHING. WAITING. WARNING.

SECTION 2   Armed & Ready

> James 4:1 From whence come wars and fightings among you? come they not hence, even of your lusts that war in your members? 2 Ye lust, and have not: ye kill, and desire to have, and cannot obtain: ye fight and war, yet ye have not, because ye ask not. 3 Ye ask, and receive not, because ye ask amiss, that ye may consume it upon your lusts. 4 Ye adulterers and adulteresses, know ye not that the friendship of the world is enmity with God? whosoever therefore will be a friend of the world is the enemy of God. 5 Do ye think that the scripture saith in vain, The spirit that dwelleth in us lusteth to envy? 6 But he giveth more grace. Wherefore he saith, God resisteth the proud, but giveth grace unto the humble. 7 Submit yourselves therefore to God. Resist the devil, and he will flee from you. 8 Draw nigh to God, and he will draw nigh to you. Cleanse your hands, ye sinners; and purify your hearts, ye double minded. 9 Be afflicted, and mourn, and weep: let your laughter be turned to mourning, and your joy to heaviness. 10 Humble yourselves in the sight of the Lord, and he shall lift you up. 11 ¶ Speak not evil one of another, brethren. He that speaketh evil of his brother, and judgeth his brother, speaketh evil of the law, and judgeth the law: but if thou judge the law, thou art not a doer of the law, but a judge.

31.	Question:	In the spaces on the next page, write out the questions asked in this scripture passage. Then, summarize the answer given.
	Answer:	i.

		ii.	
		iii.	

Galatians 6:1 Brethren, if a man be overtaken in a fault, ye which are spiritual, restore such an one in the spirit of meekness; considering thyself, lest thou also be tempted. 2 Bear ye one another's burdens, and so fulfil the law of Christ. 3 For if a man think himself to be something, when he is nothing, he deceiveth himself. 4 But let every man prove his own work, and then shall he have rejoicing in himself alone, and not in another. 5 For every man shall bear his own burden. 6 Let him that is taught in the word communicate unto him that teacheth in all good things. 7 Be not deceived; God is not mocked: for whatsoever a man soweth, that shall he also reap. 8 For he that soweth to his flesh shall of the flesh reap corruption; but he that soweth to the Spirit shall of the Spirit reap life everlasting. 9 And let us not be weary in well doing: for in due season we shall reap, if we faint not.			
32.	Question:	What does verse 1 tell believers to do?	
	Answer:		

WATCHING. WAITING. WARNING.

SECTION 2   Armed & Ready

33.	Question:	Of what shall believers be aware? (vs 1)
	Answer:	
34.	Question:	Summarize verses 2 and 3.
	Answer:	
35.	Question:	What does verse 4 say about every man?
	Answer:	
36.	Question:	What does verse 5 tell us?
	Answer:	
37.	Question:	What should the learned do? (vs 6)
	Answer:	

38.	Question:	Describe what verse 7 says about God and man.
	Answer:	
39.	Question:	Verse 8 speaks of a natural man and a spiritual man. What does it say about these?
	Answer:	
40.	Question:	Summarize verse 9.
	Answer:	
41.	Question:	Do you see any connection in this entire passage with "watching"? Explain your answer.

WATCHING. WAITING. WARNING.

SECTION 2 — Armed & Ready

	Answer:

42. Let's say a believer decided to obey Yeshua's command to watch and pray. Describe the necessary relationship between God and that believer.

44. Do you think you have that type of a relationship with God? Explain your answer.

WATCHING. WAITING. WARNING.

SECTION 2 Armed & Ready

PRECIOUS MOMENTS RECAP

45.	QUESTION:	Review this workbook chapter. Pick out the scriptures that spoke to you the most. Write at least one of those scriptures in the space below.
	ANSWER:	
46.	QUESTION:	What specific truth from the scriptures you studied in this workbook chapter speaks to you. Write that truth in the space below.
	ANSWER:	

		(continue your answer here)
47.	QUESTION:	Think of how you can apply this scripture to your life. Enter those thoughts in the space below.
	ANSWER:	

CHAPTER 5 – Tactical Training

Prepare your heart for this Chapter, as you have other Chapters ... *with prayer!*

***

Please read the following scriptures and answer the questions.

Matthew 22: 37 Jesus said unto him, Thou shalt love the Lord thy God with all thy heart, and with all thy soul, and with all thy mind. 38 This is the first and great commandment. 39 And the second is like unto it, Thou shalt love thy neighbour as thyself. 40 On these two commandments hang all the law and the prophets.		
1.	Question:	According to these words of Yeshua's, what is the first and great commandment? (vs 37-38)
	Answer:	
2.	Question:	Put this commandment into your own words.
	Answer:	
3.	Question:	What is the second commandment? (vs 39)

WATCHING. WAITING. WARNING.

SECTION 2 Armed & Ready

	Answer:	
4.	Question:	Explain how you think one can fulfil that commandment?
	Answer:	
5.	Question:	What have the law and the prophets to do with these two commandments? (vs 40)
	Answer:	
6.	Question:	The commandments point towards loving God, first. Second, towards loving your neighbour. What does one have to do with the other?
	Answer:	
7.	Question:	If you "love" God, and "love" your neighbour, are you in fact your brother's keeper?

	Answer:	

Genesis 4:9 And YeHoVaH said unto Cain, Where [is] Abel thy brother? And he said, I know not: [Am] I my brother's keeper?		
8.	Question:	What question did the Lord ask Cain?
	Answer:	
9.	Question:	How did Cain respond?
	Answer:	

Genesis 4:10 And he said, What hast thou done? the voice of thy brother's blood crieth unto me from the ground. 11 And now art thou cursed from the earth, which hath opened her mouth to receive thy brother's blood from thy hand; 12 When thou tillest the ground, it shall not henceforth yield unto thee her strength; a fugitive and a vagabond shalt thou be in the earth.		
10.	Question:	What did God ask Cain in verse 10?
	Answer:	

WATCHING. WAITING. WARNING.

SECTION 2 — Armed & Ready

11.	Question:	What did God tell Cain about his brother? (vs 10)
	Answer:	
12.	Question:	What did God say to Cain in verse 11?
	Answer:	
13.	Question:	What did God say to Cain in verse 12?
	Answer:	
14.	Question:	Read your answer again for question #7. If you think any differently, or wish to add more to your comment, enter it in the space below.
	Answer:	
15.	Question:	Re-read the scripture Genesis 4:10-12. Do you think that God "watched" over Cain and Abel?
	Answer:	
16.	Question:	What did God say He heard? (vs 10)

	Answer:	
17.	Question:	Do you think God still listens or watches over the earth and its inhabitants? If so, explain your viewpoint, using scripture, if possible.
	Answer:	
18.	Question:	Do you think there will ever be a time when God will no longer watch over His people? If so, explain your viewpoint, using scripture wherever possible.
	Answer:	

WATCHING. WAITING. WARNING.

SECTION 2   Armed & Ready

Psalm 33: 16 There is no king saved by the multitude of an host: a mighty man is not delivered by much strength. 17 An horse is a vain thing for safety: neither shall he deliver any by his great strength. 18 Behold, the eye of YeHoVaH is upon them that fear him, upon them that hope in his mercy; 19 To deliver their soul from death, and to keep them alive in famine. 20 Our soul waiteth for YeHoVaH: he is our help and our shield. 21 For our heart shall rejoice in him, because we have trusted in his holy name. 22 Let thy mercy, O LORD, be upon us, according as we hope in thee.

19.	Question:	How is a king **not** saved, according to verse 16?
	Answer:	
20.	Question:	How is a mighty man **not** delivered? (vs 16)
	Answer:	
21.	Question:	What does it say about the horse in verse 17?
	Answer:	
22.	Question:	These verses say how one is not delivered. What do you think the Psalmist wants the reader to learn? (vs 16 & 17)

	Answer:	
23.	Question:	What does verse 18 say about the Lord?
	Answer:	
24.	Question:	What does verse 19 relate regarding the Lord?
	Answer:	
25.	Question:	What does verse 20 declare?
	Answer:	
26.	Question:	Of what does verse 21 speak?
	Answer:	
Instruction:		Read this scripture passage one more time, highlight verses 16 to 17 in one colour, and verse 19 to 22 in another colour.
27.	Question:	Does verse 16 and 17 relate to verse 18? If so, how? If not, why not?

WATCHING. WAITING. WARNING.

SECTION 2 Armed & Ready

	Answer:	
28.	Question:	Does verse 19 to 22 relate to verse 18? If so, how? If not, why not?
	Answer:	

Mark 13: 28 ¶ Now learn a parable of the fig tree[22]; When her branch is yet tender, and putteth forth leaves, ye know that summer is near: 29 So ye in like manner, when ye shall see these things come to pass[23], know that it is nigh, even at the doors. 30 Verily I say unto you, that this generation shall not pass, till all these things be done. 31 Heaven and earth shall pass away: but my words shall not pass away. 32 But of that day and that hour knoweth no man, no, not the angels which are in heaven, neither the Son, but the Father. 33 Take ye heed, watch and pray: for ye know not when the time is.

29.	Question:	How does this parable begin, e.g. what is to be gained by listening to it? (verse 28)

---

[22] Many people teach this parable in reference to Israel. For this Bible Study, use its first application, which would be to the disciples, as Yeshua taught them.

[23] These are events Yeshua taught in earlier verses, prior to this parable. If you are unfamiliar with them, take your Bible and read the verses before and after!

	Answer:	
30.	Question:	What tells you the summer is near? (vs 28)
	Answer:	
31.	Question:	What value is there is observing the fig tree? (vs 29)
	Answer:	
32.	Question:	What does verse 30 tell you?
	Answer:	
33.	Question:	What does verse 31 tell you about Yeshua's words?
	Answer:	

WATCHING. WAITING. WARNING.

SECTION 2   Armed & Ready

34.	Comment:	Verse 32 refers to the time of the end, as Yeshua described in earlier verses.
	Question:	What does verse 32 say about that day?
	Answer:	
35.	Question:	What does verse 33 tell you to do and why?
	Answer:	

Mark 13: 34 For the Son of man is as a man taking a far journey, who left his house, and gave authority to his servants, and to every man his work, and commanded the porter to watch. 35 Watch ye therefore: for ye know not when the master of the house cometh, at even, or at midnight, or at the cockcrowing, or in the morning: 36 Lest coming suddenly he find you sleeping. 37 And what I say unto you I say unto all, Watch.

36.	Question:	Verse 34 begins another parable. To whom does this parable refer? (vs 34)
	Answer:	
37.	Question:	Describe the parable in verse 34 using your own words.

	Answer:	
38.	Question:	What command is given in verse 34?
	Answer:	
39.	Question:	What command does Yeshua give in verse 35?
	Answer:	
40.	Question:	Why should one watch? (vs 35 & 36)
	Answer:	
41.	Question:	To whom does Yeshua's command apply?
	Answer:	
42.	Question:	Are "you" included in that command? Explain your reasoning!

WATCHING. WAITING. WARNING.

SECTION 2 — Armed & Ready

	Answer:	

2 Peter 3: 9 ¶ The Lord is not slack concerning his promise, as some men count slackness; but is longsuffering to us-ward, not willing that any should perish, but that all should come to repentance. 10 But the day of the Lord will come as a thief in the night; in the which the heavens shall pass away with a great noise, and the elements shall melt with fervent heat, the earth also and the works that are therein shall be burned up."

43.	Question:	What does verse 9 say about the Lord?
	Answer:	
44.	Question:	How do some men count a delay?
	Answer:	
45.	Question:	Why is God longsuffering (patient)? (vs 9)
	Answer:	Reason # 1
		Reason # 2

46.	Question:	What day is spoken about in verse 10?
	Answer:	
47.	Question:	How does Yeshua describe that day? (vs 10)
	Answer:	

2 Peter 3: 11 ¶ Seeing then that all these things shall be dissolved, what manner of persons ought ye to be in all holy conversation[24] and godliness, 12 Looking for and hasting unto the coming of the day of God, wherein the heavens being on fire shall be dissolved, and the elements shall melt with fervent heat? 13 Nevertheless we, according to his promise, look for new heavens and a new earth, wherein dwelleth righteousness. 14 Wherefore, beloved, seeing that ye look for such things, be diligent that ye may be found of him in peace, without spot, and blameless.

48.	Comment:	Verse 11 speaks of "all these things". It refers to verse 10, which is referred to in the previous scripture.
	Question:	What type of a person should we be, according to verse 11?
	Answer:	
49.	Question:	For what should a believer look? (vs 12)
	Answer:	

---

[24] This KJV word means behaviour.

WATCHING. WAITING. WARNING.

SECTION 2 — Armed & Ready

50.	Question:	What day is mentioned in verse 12?
	Answer:	
51.	Question:	What shall happen on that day? (vs 12)
	Answer:	
52.	Question:	Verse 13 relates a promise of God. What is that promise?
	Answer:	
53.	Question:	What are we therefore to do? (vs 14)
	Answer:	
54.	Question:	How are we to be found when He appears? (vs 14)
	Answer:	(continue your answer here)

Chapter 5   Tactical Training

55. Write, in the space below, *a recap* of what you think Peter tells those recipients of his letter.

56. In 2 Peter 3:13, we are told, *"Nevertheless we, according to his promise, look for new heavens and a new earth, wherein dwelleth righteousness."*. Why do you think, when we know this earth and all its elements will one day pass away, it is good to look for a new heaven and a new earth?

WATCHING. WAITING. WARNING.

SECTION 2   Armed & Ready

58. **PERSONAL QUESTION:** Do you take Peter's advise? In other words, today, at this point in time, are you looking for new heavens and a new earth? If yes, explain why. If not, explain why not, or if you think you need an attitude adjustment here, explain why and what you can do about it.

Chapter 5　　　　　　　　　　　　　　　　　　　　　Tactical Training

PRECIOUS MOMENTS RECAP

59.	QUESTION:	Review this workbook chapter. Pick out the scriptures that spoke to you the most. Write at least one of those scriptures in the space below.
	ANSWER:	
60.	QUESTION:	What specific truth from the scriptures you studied in this workbook chapter speaks to you. Write that truth in the space below.
	ANSWER:	

WATCHING. WAITING. WARNING.

SECTION 2   Armed & Ready

		(continue your answer here)
61.	QUESTION:	Think of how you can apply this scripture to your life. Enter those thoughts in the space below.
	62. ANSWER:	

PRAYER BOOK ASSIGNMENT

Turn to the Prayer Book. Find the Section entitled, "Watching – A Watchman's Arms. In that section you will find an introduction and five prayers.

62. Read the Introduction. Summarize the Introduction and the scriptures that spoke to you in the space below.

63. Read "A Watchman's Place of Abiding". Summarize the prayer and the scriptures that spoke to you in the provided space.

WATCHING. WAITING. WARNING.

SECTION 2 — Armed & Ready

64. Read "A Watchman's Armour". Summarize the prayer and the scriptures that spoke to you in the provided space.

65. Read "A Watchman's Readiness". Summarize the prayer and the scriptures that spoke to you in the provided space.

Prayer Book Assignment

66. Read "A Watchman's Personal Prayer". Summarize the prayer and the scriptures that spoke to you in the provided space.

67. Read "A Watchman's Prayer for the Lost". Summarize the prayer and the scriptures that spoke to you in the provided space.

SECTION 2 — WATCHING. WAITING. WARNING. — Armed & Ready

ALL UNACCREDITED STUDENTS:

Go ahead and move on to the next part of the book.

Prayer Book Assignment

ALL STUDENTS IN THE DEGREE PROGRAM

Before moving on, you must complete your reports and do your exam.

SPECIFICS OF DEGREE GRADING	%
Online Course Audio Completion Acknowledgement...........................	7
Course Completion Acknowledgement...	2
Workbook Completion Acknowledgement...	5
Workbook Chapter Reviews	12
Prayer Book Reviews...	6
Section Review Form...	12
Personal Testimony of your spiritual benefit from this course................	8
All of the above must be submitted before scheduling the final exam	52
Online Course Final Exam..	48
TOTAL	100
Passing Grade to receive credits...	69
NOTE: Grade to continue taking courses for your degree	75

See the website for the forms to complete your reports.

COURSE 404
WATCHING. WAITING. WARNING.

SECTION 2 –

Armed & Ready continued

WAITING

CHAPTER 6 – Targeted Solutions

Don't forget to precede this Chapter with prayer, too!

***

Read the following scriptures and answer the questions.

Genesis 15:1 ¶ After these things the word of YeHoVaH came unto Abram in a vision, saying, Fear not, Abram: I am thy shield, and thy exceeding great reward.		
1.	Comment:	Verse 1 begins with these words, "after these things". This refers to events happening in a previous chapter of Genesis.
	Question:	Take your Bible and look up the main event which Genesis 14 records. Summarize it in the space below.
	Answer:	

WATCHING. WAITING. WARNING.

SECTION 2   Armed & Ready

2.	Comment:	The man named Abram was given a new name by God. That name you probably know: *Abraham.*
	Question:	Why do you think the Lord said to Abram, "Fear not, Abram, I am thy shield and thy exceeding great reward." HINT: Remember the event in Genesis Chapter 14.
	Answer:	

Genesis 15:2 ¶ And Abram said, Lord GOD, what wilt thou give me, seeing I go childless, and the steward of my house is this Eliezer of Damascus? 3 And Abram said, Behold, to me thou hast given no seed: and, lo, one born in my house is mine heir. 4 And, behold, the word of YeHoVaH came unto him, saying, This shall not be thine heir; but he that shall come forth out of thine own bowels shall be thine heir. 5 And he brought him forth abroad, and said, Look now toward heaven, and tell the stars, if thou be able to number them: and he said unto him, So shall thy seed be. 6 And he believed in YeHoVaH; and he counted it to him for righteousness.

3.	Question:	Abram asks God a question. What is that question? (vs 2)
	Answer:	

4.	Question:	Why did Abram mention his steward (servant) Eliezer of Damascus? (vs 2-3)
	Answer:	

5.	Question:	How did the Lord respond to Abram? (vs 4)
	Answer:	
6.	Question:	Put God's words to Abram in modern English. (This is for ease of understanding.)
	Answer:	
7.	Question:	What did God say and do with Abram in verse 5?
	Answer:	
8.	Question:	How did Abram respond to the Lord? (vs 6)
	Answer:	
9.	Question:	How did the Lord respond, then, to Abram? (vs 6)
	Answer:	

WATCHING. WAITING. WARNING.

SECTION 2   Armed & Ready

10.	Question:	Why do you think the author of Genesis, Moses, saw it fitting to tell us the information in verse 6?
	Answer:	

Genesis 15: 7 ¶ And he said unto him, I am YeHoVaH that brought thee out of Ur of the Chaldees, to give thee this land to inherit it. 8 And he said, Lord GOD, whereby shall I know that I shall inherit it?

11.	Question:	What does God tell Abram about Himself? (vs 7)
	Answer:	
12.	Question:	What does the Lord promise Abram? (vs 7)
	Answer:	
13.	Question:	How did Abram respond to God? (vs 8)

	Answer:	

Genesis 15: 9 And he said unto him, Take me an heifer of three years old, and a she goat of three years old, and a ram of three years old, and a turtledove, and a young pigeon. 10 And he took unto him all these, and divided them in the midst, and laid each piece one against another: but the birds divided he not. 11 And when the fowls came down upon the carcases, Abram drove them away.

14.	Comment:	This passage continues on from the scripture in the question above. Remember verse 8 and your answer to question # 13.
	Question:	What does God say to Abram? (vs 9)
	Answer:	
15.	Question:	What does verse 10 say Abram did with these?
	Answer:	
16.	Question:	What did Abram do, according to verse 11?
	Answer:	

WATCHING. WAITING. WARNING.

SECTION 2 Armed & Ready

17. We will study this scripture in more detail later, but for now, know this passage refers to what is commonly known as "cutting covenant". Genesis 15:9 lists 5 animals. Abram was to cut the larger animals in two, and place each cut portion, side by side, in a row. The birds, not divided, were put on either end. In the *boxes and circles* below, write the names of the animals. Hint: remember, the animals were divided in two.

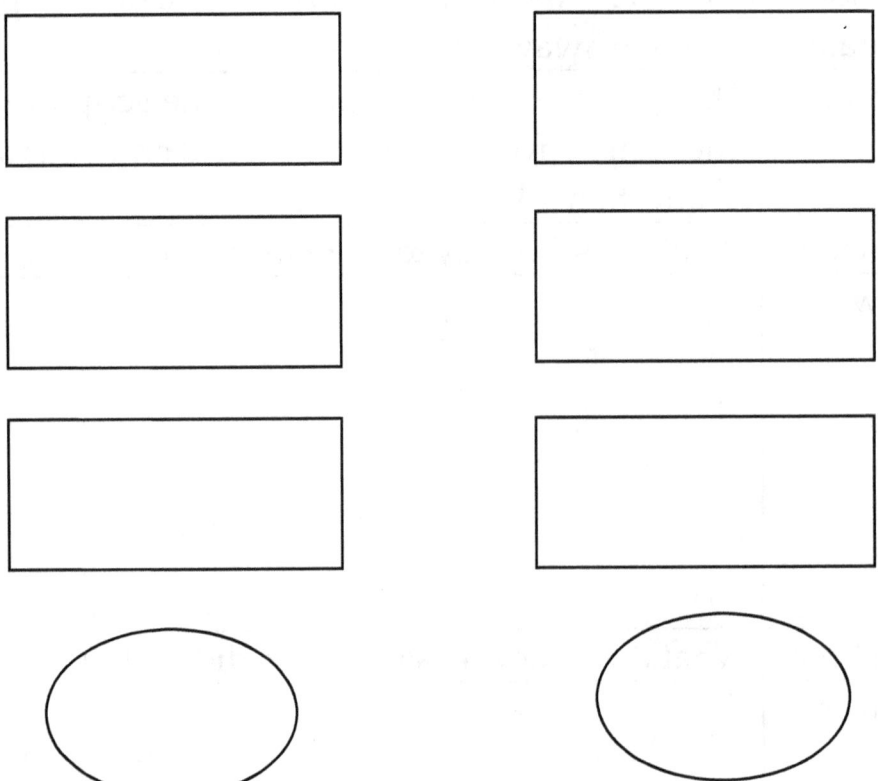

18. Why do you think Abram drove away the fowls of the air? (Hint: fowls like hawks, vultures, etc.)

19. Do you think there is a spiritual lesson to be gleaned from Abraham's action with the fowls of the air? If so, what?. If not, why not?

Genesis 15: 12 ¶ And when the sun was going down, a deep sleep fell upon Abram; and, lo, an horror of great darkness fell upon him. 13 And he said unto Abram, Know of a surety that thy seed shall be a stranger in a land that is not theirs, and shall serve them; and they shall afflict them four hundred years; 14 And also that nation, whom they shall serve, will I judge: and afterward shall they come out with great substance. 15 And thou shalt go to thy fathers in peace; thou shalt be buried in a good old age. 16 But in the fourth generation they shall come hither again: for the iniquity of the Amorites is not yet full.

20.	Question:	What time of day was it as stated in verse 12?
	Answer:	
21.	Question:	According to verse 12, two things fell upon Abram. What was the first thing?
	Answer:	
22.	Question:	What was the 2nd thing that "fell" upon Abram? (vs 12)
	Answer:	
23.	Question:	What did God say to Abram? (vs 13)

WATCHING. WAITING. WARNING.

SECTION 2 — Armed & Ready

	Answer:	
24.	Question:	What does verse 14 say God would do?
	Answer:	
25.	Question:	What happens to Abram's seed? (vs 14)
	Answer:	
26.	Question:	What happens to Abram according to verse 15?
	Answer:	
27.	Question:	What does God say about the 4th generation[25]? (vs 16)
	Answer:	
28.	Question:	Why would God not deal with the Amorites sooner? (vs 16)
	Answer:	

---

[25] This 4th generation refers to Abram's descendants.

Genesis 15: 17 ¶ And it came to pass, that, when the sun went down, and it was dark, behold a smoking furnace, and a burning lamp that passed between those pieces. 18 In the same day YeHoVaH made a covenant with Abram, saying, Unto thy seed have I given this land, from the river of Egypt unto the great river, the river Euphrates: 19 The Kenites, and the Kenizzites, and the Kadmonites, 20 And the Hittites, and the Perizzites, and the Rephaims, 21 And the Amorites, and the Canaanites, and the Girgashites, and the Jebusites.		
29.	Question:	What time of day is described in verse 17?
	Answer:	
30.	Question:	Is this the same time of day as mentioned in the scripture verses mentioned before Question # 20 (Genesis 15:12)
	Answer:	
31.	Comment:	To understand what is meant by "between the pieces", refer to your diagram on Genesis 15: 9. (Where you filled in the names of the animals.)
	Question:	What passed between the pieces? (vs 17)
	Answer:	
32.	Question:	What do you think that represented?
	Answer:	
33.	Question:	What does verse 18 tell us that God did?

	Answer:	
34.	Question:	What does it say about land in verse 18?
	Answer:	
35.	Question:	Without going into great detail, see if you can summarize the terms of this covenant as found in Genesis 15. *(The covenant continues on in other chapters, so just outline the terms you see here.)*
	Answer:	

Chapter 6 — Targeted Solutions

> Galatians 4:22 For it is written, that Abraham had two sons, the one by a bondmaid, the other by a freewoman. 23 But he [who was] of the bondwoman was born after the flesh; but he of the freewoman [was] by promise. 24 Which things are an allegory: for these are the two covenants; the one from the mount Sinai, which gendereth to bondage, 25 which is Agar. For this Agar is mount Sinai in Arabia, and answereth to Jerusalem which now is, and is in bondage with her children. 26 But Jerusalem which is above is free, which is the mother of us all. 27 For it is written, Rejoice, thou barren that bearest not; break forth and cry, thou that travailest not: for the desolate hath many more children than she which hath an husband. 28 Now we, brethren, as Isaac was, are the children of promise.

36.	Comment:	Abraham had two sons. Ishmael and Isaac. Ishmael was born of Hagar, a bondmaid. Isaac was born of Sarah, Abraham's legal wife, who was a freewoman.
	Question:	What does verse 23 say about the two sons?
	Answer:	
37.	Question:	Put verse 24 into your own words.
	Answer:	
38.	Question:	Which covenant came from Mount Sinai? (Hint: think of Moses and the 10 commandments.)
	Answer:	
39.	Question:	What does it say about Jerusalem in verse 25?

WATCHING. WAITING. WARNING.

SECTION 2 — Armed & Ready

	Answer:	
40.	Question:	What is the Jerusalem from above? (vs 26)
	Answer:	
41.	Question:	Outline the paradox in verse 27.
	Answer:	
42.	Question:	What does verse 28 tell us? (Remember, this letter from Paul is to New Covenant believers!)
	Answer:	

Galatians 4: 29 But as then he that was born after the flesh persecuted him that was born after the Spirit, even so it is now. 30 Nevertheless what saith the scripture? Cast out the bondwoman and her son: for the son of the bondwoman shall not be heir with the son of the freewoman.

43.	Comment:	*"He that was born after the flesh"* refers to Ishmael. *"Him that was born after the Spirit"* refers to Isaac.
	Question:	What does verse 29 say Ishmael did to Isaac?
	Answer:	

44.	Question:	Who was to be cast out? (verse 30)
	Answer:	

45.	Question:	Why were they to be cast out? (verse 30)
	Answer:	

46.	Comment:	Looking back to earlier verses, (Galatians 4: 22-24) these events are a real to life demonstration, presenting us with an allegory.
	Question:	What is the allegory here? (vs 30)
	Answer:	(continue your answer here)

WATCHING. WAITING. WARNING.

SECTION 2   **Armed & Ready**

1 John 2: 1 ¶ My little children, these things write I unto you, that ye sin not. And if any man sin, we have an advocate with the Father, Jesus Christ the righteous: 2 And he is the propitiation for our sins: and not for ours only, but also for the sins of the whole world. 3 ¶ And hereby we do know that we know him, if we keep his commandments. 4 He that saith, I know him, and keepeth not his commandments, is a liar, and the truth is not in him. 5 But whoso keepeth his word, in him verily is the love of God perfected: hereby know we that we are in him. 6 He that saith he abideth in him ought himself also so to walk, even as he walked.

47.	Question:	What happens if a man sins? (vs 1)
	Answer:	
48.	Question:	What is said of this advocate? (vs 2)
	Answer:	
49.	Question:	How does verse 3 tell us that we know Him?
	Answer:	
50.	Question:	What does verse 4 say about a liar?
	Answer:	

51.	Question:	What does it say about those who keep God's word? (vs 5)
	Answer:	
52.	Question:	What does one do who truly abides in Him? (vs 6)
	Answer:	

2 Timothy 2: 15 Study to shew thyself approved unto God, a workman that needeth not to be ashamed, rightly dividing the word of truth. 16 But shun profane and vain babblings: for they will increase unto more ungodliness. 17 And their word will eat as doth a canker: of whom is Hymenaeus and Philetus; 18 Who concerning the truth have erred, saying that the resurrection is past already; and overthrow the faith of some. 19 ¶ Nevertheless the foundation of God standeth sure, having this seal, The Lord knoweth them that are his. And, Let every one that nameth the name of Christ depart from iniquity.

53.	Question:	What does verse 15 say to do?
	Answer:	

WATCHING. WAITING. WARNING.

SECTION 2 — Armed & Ready

54.	Question:	What are we to shun and why? (vs 16)
	Answer:	
55.	Question:	What does verse 17 say about Hymenaeus and Philetus?
	Answer:	
56.	Question:	What does verse 18 tell us they did and said?
	Answer:	
57.	Question:	a) How does the foundation of God stand? b) What seals it? (verse 19)
	Answer:	a)
		b)
58.	Question:	What should everyone do who names of the name of Yeshua?
	Answer:	
59.	Question:	What measuring stick do you think the Lord gave us to see whether we have departed from iniquity?
	Answer:	

Hebrews 11: 13 These all died in faith[26], not having received the promises, but having seen them afar off, and were persuaded of them, and embraced them, and confessed that they were strangers and pilgrims on the earth. 14 For they that say such things declare plainly that they seek a country. 15 And truly, if they had been mindful of that country from whence they came out, they might have had opportunity to have returned. 16 But now they desire a better [country], that is, an heavenly: wherefore God is not ashamed to be called their God: for he hath prepared for them a city.

60.	Question:	Did those who died in faith, mentioned in verse 13, receive the promises? *(A yes or no answer is OK here!)*
	Answer:	
61.	Question:	What attitude does verse 13 say they had towards the promises?
	Answer:	
62.	Question:	What does verse 14 say about those with that attitude?

---

[26] "These all died in faith", refers to the previous chapter. If you are not familiar with this, take out your Bible and read chapter 11.

WATCHING. WAITING. WARNING.

SECTION 2 — Armed & Ready

	Answer:	
63.	Question:	What does verse 15 say about that attitude?
	Answer:	
64.	Question:	What does verse 16 say they desired?
	Answer:	
65.	Question:	What does God think about these ones, and what has He done for them? (vs 16)
	Answer:	

Chapter 6 — Targeted Solutions

Ephesians 1: 13 In whom ye[27] also [trusted], after that ye heard the word of truth, the gospel of your salvation: in whom also after that ye believed, ye were sealed with that holy Spirit of promise, 14 Which is the earnest[28] of our inheritance until the redemption of the purchased possession, unto the praise of his glory."

66.	Question:	What does verse 13 tell us about "being sealed"?
	Answer:	
67.	Question:	What is the down payment (earnest)? (vs 14)
	Answer:	
68.	Question:	When is the remainder received? (vs 14)
	Answer:	
69.	Question:	What does this bring to God? (vs 14)
	Answer:	

---

[27] This refers to believers (Remember: if you are not familiar with this passage, look up some surrounding verses, before and after!)
[28] This word means down payment

WATCHING. WAITING. WARNING.

SECTION 2   Armed & Ready

70. Thus far, in this course, what have you learned about God? (If you need more space, use another sheet of paper.)

PRECIOUS MOMENTS RECAP

71.	QUESTION:	Review this workbook chapter. Pick out the scriptures that spoke to you the most. Write at least one of those scriptures in the space below.
	ANSWER:	
72.	QUESTION:	What specific truth from the scriptures you studied in this workbook chapter speaks to you. Write that truth in the space below.
	ANSWER:	(continue your answer here)

WATCHING. WAITING. WARNING.

SECTION 2   Armed & Ready

73.	QUESTION:	Think of how you can apply this scripture to your life. Enter those thoughts in the space below.
	ANSWER:	

CHAPTER 7 – Tactical Avoidances

Remember: precede this Chapter with prayer!

***

Please read the scriptures and answer the questions.

2 Corinthians 10: 1 ¶ Now I Paul myself beseech you by the meekness and gentleness of Christ, who in presence [am] base among you, but being absent am bold toward you: 2 But I beseech [you], that I may not be bold when I am present with that confidence, wherewith I think to be bold against some, which think of us as if we walked according to the flesh. 3 For though we walk in the flesh, we do not war after the flesh: 4 (For the weapons of our warfare [are] not carnal, but mighty through God to the pulling down of strong holds;) 5 Casting down imaginations, and every high thing that exalteth itself against the knowledge of God, and bringing into captivity every thought to the obedience of Christ; 6 And having in a readiness to revenge all disobedience, when your obedience is fulfilled."		
1.	Question:	What does Paul say about himself in verse 1 and why?
	Answer:	
2.	Question:	What does Paul say in verse 2?

WATCHING. WAITING. WARNING.

SECTION 2　　　　　　　　　　　　　　　　　　　　　　　　　Armed & Ready

	Answer:	
3.	Question:	What does Paul say in verse 3?
	Answer:	
4.	Question:	Do you think the message in verse 3 is an important one for Paul's listeners to remember?
	Answer:	
5.	Question:	What does Paul say about weapons in verse 4?
	Answer:	
6.	Question:	What is one to do according to verse 5 and 6?
	Answer:	

2 Chronicles 20: 15 And he said, Hearken ye, all Judah, and ye inhabitants of Jerusalem, and thou king Jehoshaphat, Thus saith YeHoVaH unto you, Be not afraid nor dismayed by reason of this great multitude; for the battle is not yours, but God's. 16 To morrow go ye down against them: behold, they come up by the cliff of Ziz; and ye shall find them at the end of the brook, before the wilderness of Jeruel. 17 Ye shall not need to fight in this battle: set yourselves, stand ye still, and see the salvation of YeHoVaH with you, O Judah and Jerusalem: fear not, nor be dismayed; to morrow go out against them: for YeHoVaH will be with you. 18 And Jehoshaphat bowed his head with his face to the ground: and all Judah and the inhabitants of Jerusalem fell before YeHoVaH, worshipping YeHoVaH. 19 And the Levites, of the children of the Kohathites, and of the children of the Korhites, stood up to praise YeHoVaH God of Israel with a loud voice on high. 20 ¶ And they rose early in the morning, and went forth into the wilderness of Tekoa: and as they went forth, Jehoshaphat stood and said, Hear me, O Judah, and ye inhabitants of Jerusalem; Believe in YeHoVaH your God, so shall ye be established; believe his prophets, so shall ye prosper. 21 And when he had consulted with the people, he appointed singers unto YeHoVaH, and that should praise the beauty of holiness, as they went out before the army, and to say, Praise YeHoVaH; for his mercy endureth for ever. 22 And when they began to sing and to praise, YeHoVaH set ambushments against the children of Ammon, Moab, and mount Seir, which were come against Judah; and they were smitten.

7.	Question:	Recap the main theme of verse 15 to 16.
	Answer:	
8.	Question:	Using a highlighter, highlight verse 17. Then write a recap of that verse in the space below.
	Answer:	

WATCHING. WAITING. WARNING.

SECTION 2   Armed & Ready

9.	Question:	What do verses 18 to 19 tell us?
	Answer:	
10.	Question:	Recap the words of Jehoshaphat in verse 20.
	Answer:	
11.	Question:	Recap verse 21.
	Answer:	
12.	Question:	Put verse 22 in your own words.
	Answer:	
13.	Question:	What do you think we can learn from this portion of scripture?

	Answer:	

John 15:1 ¶ I am the true vine, and my Father is the husbandman. 2 Every branch in me that beareth not fruit he taketh away: and every branch that beareth fruit, he purgeth it, that it may bring forth more fruit. 3 Now ye are clean through the word which I have spoken unto you. 4 Abide in me, and I in you. As the branch cannot bear fruit of itself, except it abide in the vine; no more can ye, except ye abide in me. 5 I am the vine, ye are the branches: He that abideth in me, and I in him, the same bringeth forth much fruit: for without me ye can do nothing. 6 If a man abide not in me, he is cast forth as a branch, and is withered; and men gather them, and cast them into the fire, and they are burned. 7 If ye abide in me, and my words abide in you, ye shall ask what ye will, and it shall be done unto you. 8 Herein is my Father glorified, that ye bear much fruit; so shall ye be my disciples.

14. Yeshua compared Himself to a vine and believers to its branches. In the space provided, draw a picture of what you believe Yeshua says to His followers. (John 15:1-8)

WATCHING. WAITING. WARNING.
SECTION 2   Armed & Ready

15. In the picture you drew above, draw a smiley face somewhere on one of the branches. Near by the smiley face, put your name!

16. John 15:6 says what happens if a branch does not abide in Yeshua? Recap what Yeshua says happens and then draw a picture of that might look like!

17. Verse 7 says "If ye abide in me, and my words abide in you, ye shall ask what ye will, and it shall be done unto you. " Put this verse into your own words.

WATCHING. WAITING. WARNING.

SECTION 2   Armed & Ready

18.   How is the Father glorified? (Vs 8)

19.   On a scale of 1 to 20, grade your success in abiding in Yeshua. If you feel you have room for improvement, be sure to add that comment as well!

1 Corinthians 6: 19 What? know ye not that your body is the temple of the Holy Ghost which is in you, which ye have of God, and you are not your own? 20 For ye are bought with a price: therefore glorify God in your body, and in your spirit, which are God's.		
20.	Question:	What is the message in verse 19?
	Answer:	

21.	Question:	What does it mean in verse 19 by the words, "you are not your own?"
	Answer:	

22.	Question:	Why are we not our own? (vs 20)
	Answer:	

23.	Question:	How should we glorify God?
	Answer:	

24.	Question:	Who owns the body and spirit?
	Answer:	

WATCHING. WAITING. WARNING.

SECTION 2   Armed & Ready

Romans 11:1 ¶ I say then, Hath God cast away his people? God forbid. For I also am an Israelite, of the seed of Abraham, of the tribe of Benjamin. 2 God hath not cast away his people which he foreknew. Wot ye not what the scripture saith of Elias? how he maketh intercession to God against Israel, saying, 3 Lord, they have killed thy prophets, and digged down thine altars; and I am left alone, and they seek my life. 4 But what saith the answer of God unto him? I have reserved to myself seven thousand men, who have not bowed the knee to the image of Baal. 5 Even so then at this present time also there is a remnant according to the election of grace. 6 And if by grace, then is it no more of works: otherwise grace is no more grace. But if it be of works, then is it no more grace: otherwise work is no more work. 7 What then? Israel hath not obtained that which he seeketh for; but the election hath obtained it, and the rest were blinded 8 (According as it is written, God hath given them the spirit of slumber, eyes that they should not see, and ears that they should not hear;) unto this day.

25.	Question:	What question does Paul ask in verse 1?
	Answer:	
26.	Question:	How does Paul answer that question in verses 1 and 2?
	Answer:	
27.	Comment:	In verse 2, Paul begins to speak about Elias. This is the Greek name for Elijah.
	Question:	What does verse 2 say of Elijah?
	Answer:	

28.	Question:	What plight does Elijah describe in verse 3?
	Answer:	
29.	Question:	How did God respond to Elijah? (vs 4)
	Answer:	
30.	Question:	What does Paul say about the remnant in verse 5?
	Answer:	
31.	Question:	What does verse 6 say about grace and works?
	Answer:	
32.	Comment:	The "election" (vs 7) are those who are born again in Messiah. "Israel" here refers to those who did not receive Yeshua.
	Question:	What happened to those who did not receive Yeshua? (vs 7)
	Answer:	
33.	Question:	According to verse 8, what does God give to them?

WATCHING. WAITING. WARNING.

SECTION 2   Armed & Ready

	Answer:	
34.	Question:	This passage is somewhat hard to understand. If you have any questions, write them in the space below.
	Answer:	

Isaiah 29: 7 And the multitude of all the nations that fight against Ariel[29], even all that fight against her and her munition, and that distress her, shall be as a dream of a night vision. 8 It shall even be as when an hungry man dreameth, and, behold, he eateth; but he awaketh, and his soul is empty: or as when a thirsty man dreameth, and, behold, he drinketh; but he awaketh, and, behold, he is faint, and his soul hath appetite: so shall the multitude of all the nations be, that fight against mount Zion

35.	Question:	What does verse 7 say regarding nations?
	Answer:	
36.	Question:	What happens to those that distress her? (vs 8)
	Answer:	

Isaiah 29:9 ¶ Stay yourselves, and wonder; cry ye out, and cry: they are drunken, but not with wine; they stagger, but not with strong drink. 10

---

[29] This is another name for Jerusalem

Chapter 7 — Tactical Avoidances

> For YeHoVaH hath poured out upon you the spirit of deep sleep, and hath closed your eyes: the prophets and your rulers, the seers hath he covered. 11 And the vision of all is become unto you as the words of a book that is sealed, which men deliver to one that is learned, saying, Read this, I pray thee: and he saith, I cannot; for it is sealed: 12 And the book is delivered to him that is not learned, saying, Read this, I pray thee: and he saith, I am not learned.

37.	Question:	Describe the happenings in verse 9?
	Answer:	

38.	Question:	What does verse 10 say the Lord did?
	Answer:	

39.	Question:	What has the vision become? (vs 11)
	Answer:	

40.	Question:	Can learned or unlearned people read the book? Why or why not? (vs 11-12)
	Answer:	

WATCHING. WAITING. WARNING.

SECTION 2   Armed & Ready

Isaiah 29:13 Wherefore the Lord said, Forasmuch as this people draw near me with their mouth, and with their lips do honour me, but have removed their heart far from me, and their fear toward me is taught by the precept of men: 14 Therefore, behold, I will proceed to do a marvellous work among this people, even a marvellous work and a wonder: for the wisdom of their wise men shall perish, and the understanding of their prudent men shall be hid.		
41.	Question:	What does verse 13 tells us about the people?
	Answer:	
42.	Question:	How did they teach the fear of God, according to verse 13?
	Answer:	
43.	Question:	What does God proceed to do? (vs 14)
	Answer:	
44.	Question:	What happens to the wisdom of the wise man? (vs 14)
	Answer:	

45.	Question:	What happens to the understanding of their prudent men? (vs 14)
	Answer:	

46. Re-Read from Isaiah 29:7-14, pages 132 to 134.
    a. Recap what happens to those who fight against Ariel (Jerusalem)
    b. Compare what happens to them, with what happens to those who honour God with only lip service.

WATCHING. WAITING. WARNING.

SECTION 2 — Armed & Ready

Isaiah 40: 27 ¶ Why sayest thou, O Jacob[30], and speakest, O Israel, My way is hid from YeHoVaH, and my judgment is passed over from my God? 28 Hast thou not known? hast thou not heard, [that] the everlasting God, YeHoVaH, the Creator of the ends of the earth, fainteth not, neither is weary? [there is] no searching of his understanding. 29 He giveth power to the faint; and to [them that have] no might he increaseth strength. 30 Even the youths shall faint and be weary, and the young men shall utterly fall: 31 But they that wait upon YeHoVaH shall renew [their] strength; they shall mount up with wings as eagles; they shall run, and not be weary; [and] they shall walk, and not faint."

47.	Question:	What two things does Jacob (Israel) speak or say?
	Answer:	

48.	Question:	What question is asked in verse 28?
	Answer:	

49.	Question:	Who can search out God's understanding? (vs 28)
	Answer:	

50.	Question:	What does verse 29 relate about God?
	Answer:	

---

[30] Jacob is another name for Israel. Genesis 32:28 And he said, Thy name shall be called no more Jacob, but Israel: for as a prince hast thou power with God and with men, and hast prevailed.

51.	Question:	What is said of the youth in verse 30?
	Answer:	
52.	Question:	What happens to those who wait upon the Lord? (vs 31)
	Answer:	

53. What do you think it means to "wait upon the Lord?"

WATCHING. WAITING. WARNING.

SECTION 2
Armed & Ready

54. Do you think it is important to wait upon the Lord? Explain your reasons and use scripture wherever possible.

55. Using your own Bible knowledge, list at least two people who, in their situation, *did not wait* upon the Lord.

56. Using the same two people as in the question above, what happened because they *did not wait* upon the Lord?

57. Using your own Bible knowledge, list at least two people who, in their situation, *waited* upon the Lord.

58. Using the same two people as in the question above, what happened because they *waited* upon the Lord?

PRECIOUS MOMENTS RECAP

59.	QUESTION:	Review this workbook chapter. Pick out the scriptures that spoke to you the most. Write at least one of those scriptures in the space below.
	ANSWER:	
60.	QUESTION:	What specific truth from the scriptures you studied in this workbook chapter speaks to you. Write that truth in the space below.
	ANSWER:	

		(continue your answer here)
61.	QUESTION:	Think of how you can apply this scripture to your life. Enter those thoughts in the space below.
	62. ANSWER:	

WATCHING. WAITING. WARNING.

SECTION 2   Armed & Ready

PRAYER BOOK ASSIGNMENT

Turn to the Prayer Book. Find the Section entitled, "Waiting – A Watchman's Ally. In that section you will find an introduction and five prayers.

62. Read the Introduction. Summarize the Introduction and the scriptures that spoke to you in the space below.

63. Read "Ayin YeHoVaH". Summarize the prayer and the scriptures that spoke to you in the provided space.

Prayer Book Assignment

64. Read "YeHoVaH Yir'eh". Summarize the prayer and the scriptures that spoke to you in the provided space.

65. Read "YeHoVaH Tsidkenu". Summarize the prayer and the scriptures that spoke to you in the provided space.

WATCHING. WAITING. WARNING.

SECTION 2 — Armed & Ready

66. Read "El Sali". Summarize the prayer and the scriptures that spoke to you in the provided space.

67. Read "YeHoVaH Shammah". Summarize the prayer and the scriptures that spoke to you in the provided space.

WARNING

CHAPTER 8–Targeted Surveillance

Psalm 36:9 For with thee is the fountain of life: in thy light shall we see light.

***

1. As you begin this Chapter, recap some of your thoughts about the following:

Watching	
Waiting	

WATCHING. WAITING. WARNING.

SECTION 2   Armed & Ready

2. Using a dictionary, online or otherwise, look up the word "warning". Write its definition in the space below.

Read the following scriptures and answer the questions:

> Habakkuk 2:1 ¶ I will stand upon my watch, and set me upon the tower, and will watch to see what he will say unto me, and what I shall answer when I am reproved. 2 And YeHoVaH answered me, and said, Write the vision, and make it plain upon tables, that he may run that readeth it. 3 For the vision is yet for an appointed time, but at the end it shall speak, and not lie: though it tarry, wait for it; because it will surely come, it will not tarry.

3.	Question:	Where does verse 1 position Habakkuk?
	Answer:	
4.	Question:	Why was the prophet Habakkuk there? (vs 1)
	Answer:	
5.	Question:	What does Habakkuk wait for? (vs 1)
	Answer:	
6.	Question:	What content does YeHoVaH expect the prophet to do? (vs 2)

	Answer:	
7.	Question:	Why do you suppose the one who reads it must run with it?
	Answer:	
8.	Question:	Is the vision for now or later? (vs 3)
	Answer:	
9.	Question:	When will the vision speak? (vs 3)
	Answer:	
10.	Question:	What shall the vision relate? (vs 3) (Hint: opposite to the words "and not lie".
	Answer:	
11.	Question:	Regarding the vision, what does one do? (vs 3)
	Answer:	
12.	Question:	Why does one do this? (vs 3)
	Answer:	

Joel 1: 15 Alas for the day! for the day of the LORD is at hand, and as a destruction from the Almighty shall it come. 16 Is not the meat cut off

before our eyes, yea, joy and gladness from the house of our God? 17 The seed is rotten under their clods, the garners are laid desolate, the barns are broken down; for the corn is withered. 18 How do the beasts groan! the herds of cattle are perplexed, because they have no pasture; yea, the flocks of sheep are made desolate. 19 O LORD, to thee will I cry: for the fire hath devoured the pastures of the wilderness, and the flame hath burned all the trees of the field. 20 The beasts of the field cry also unto thee: for the rivers of waters are dried up, and the fire hath devoured the pastures of the wilderness. 2:1 ¶ Blow ye the trumpet in Zion, and sound an alarm in my holy mountain: let all the inhabitants of the land tremble: for the day of the LORD cometh, for it is nigh at hand;

13.	Question:	What day is mentioned in verse 15?
	Answer:	
14.	Question:	Is that day far or near? (vs 15)
	Answer:	
15.	Question:	From Whom does it come? (vs 15)
	Answer:	
16.	Question:	How does verse 15 describe the contents of that day?
	Answer:	
17.	Question:	Read verses 16 to 20. Describe the devastation.
	Answer:	
18.	Question:	To Whom does the prophet cry and why? (vs 19)
	Answer:	
19.	Question:	To Whom do the beasts of the field cry and why? (vs 20)

	Answer:	
20.	Question:	What day is spoken about in Chapter 2:1?
	Answer:	
21.	Question:	How are the people to know that day is coming? (e.g. what is the warning sound?) (vs 1)
	Answer:	
22.	Question:	Is that day near or far? (vs 1)
	Answer:	

> Joel 2:2 A day of darkness and of gloominess, a day of clouds and of thick darkness, as the morning spread upon the mountains: a great people and a strong; there hath not been ever the like, neither shall be any more after it, even to the years of many generations. 3 A fire devoureth before them; and behind them a flame burneth: the land is as the garden of Eden before them, and behind them a desolate wilderness; yea, and nothing shall escape them. 4 The appearance of them is as the appearance of horses; and as horsemen, so shall they run. 5 Like the noise of chariots on the tops of mountains shall they leap, like the noise of a flame of fire that devoureth the stubble, as a strong people set in battle array. 6 Before their face the people shall be much pained: all faces shall gather blackness. 7 They shall run like mighty men; they shall climb the wall like men of war; and they shall march every one on his ways, and they shall not break their ranks: 8 Neither shall one thrust another; they shall walk every one in his path: and when they fall upon the sword, they shall not be wounded. 9 They shall run to and fro in the city; they shall run upon the wall, they shall climb up upon the houses; they shall enter in at the windows like a thief. 10 The

SECTION 2
WATCHING. WAITING. WARNING.
Armed & Ready

earth shall quake before them; the heavens shall tremble: the sun and the moon shall be dark, and the stars shall withdraw their shining:

23.	Question:	Describe that day according to each verse:
	Answer:	Vs 2
		Vs 3
		Vs 4

		Vs 5	
		Vs 6	
		Vs 7	

		Vs 8	
		Vs 9	
		Vs 10	

Joel 2:11 And YeHoVaH shall utter his voice before his army: for his camp is very great: for he is strong that executeth his word: for the day of the LORD is great and very terrible; and who can abide it?		
24.	Question:	What does the Lord do on that day? (vs 11)
	Answer:	
25.	Question:	What does verse 11 say about His army?
	Answer:	
26.	Question:	What does verse 11 say about the one who executes His word?
	Answer:	
27.	Question:	Describe what verse 11 says about the day of the Lord.
	Answer:	
28.	Question:	What question does verse 11 ask?
	Answer:	

SECTION 2   WATCHING. WAITING. WARNING.   Armed & Ready

29. What do you think the answer might be to the question asked in verse 11?

30. How do you think you would do on such a day? Prove your viewpoint with scripture.

> Isaiah 56:10 His watchmen are blind: they are all ignorant, they are all dumb dogs, they cannot bark; sleeping, lying down, loving to slumber. 11 Yea, they are greedy dogs which can never have enough, and they are shepherds that cannot understand: they all look to their own way, every one for his gain, from his quarter. 12 Come ye, say they, I will fetch wine, and we will fill ourselves with strong drink; and to morrow shall be as this day, and much more abundant. **57**:1 The righteous perisheth, and no man

\multicolumn{3}{l}{layeth it to heart: and merciful men are taken away, none considering that the righteous is taken away from the evil to come.}
31.	Comment:	This passage speaks of those who watch God's people, but not for the sake of the Lord.
	Question:	What are these watchmen like? (vs 10)
	Answer:	
32.	Question:	Why is it a problem if a dog doesn't bark?
	Answer:	
33.	Question:	What do these watchmen in verse 1 love?
	Answer:	
34.	Question:	How does verse 11 describe these watchmen (shepherds)?
	Answer:	

SECTION 2 — WATCHING. WAITING. WARNING. — Armed & Ready

35.	Question:	What does every one of them look for? (vs 11)
	Answer:	
36.	Question:	What do they say? What do they promise? (vs 12)
	Answer:	
37.	Question:	What happens to the righteous man? (57:1)
	Answer:	
38.	Question:	Who cares about that situation? (57:1)
	Answer:	
39.	Question:	What happens to merciful men? (57:1)
	Answer:	
40.	Question:	What is it that no one considers? (57:1)
	Answer:	

41. Looking at this passage, from the opposite side, one could see the duties of a good watchmen. Summarize those duties and write them in the provided space below and on the top of the next page. .

42. What do you feel is the bottom line of:

   a. A good watchman:

   b. A bad watchman:

43. Why do you think bad watchmen incur the anger of God?

44. What qualities do you see in yourself that would make you a good watchman? What deficiencies in yourself do you think you might need to work on? Use the space below to answer the questions.

A look at your own life.

My Good Qualities	Areas of Deficiency

Give your weakness to YeHoVaH, for His help in those areas of your life! Give Him thanks for the good things He has brought about in you! Stand ready to receive His help in those areas, too, for at times, strengths pushed too far become a weakness!

PRECIOUS MOMENTS RECAP

45.	QUESTION:	Review this workbook chapter. Pick out the scriptures that spoke to you the most. Write at least one of those scriptures in the space below.
	ANSWER:	
46.	QUESTION:	What specific truth from the scriptures you studied in this workbook chapter speaks to you. Write that truth in the space below.
	ANSWER:	

		(continue your answer here)
47.	QUESTION:	Think of how you can apply this scripture to your life. Enter those thoughts in the space below.
	48. ANSWER:	

CHAPTER 9– Tactical Responses

As this is the last Chapter prior to doing this Chapter, thank God for what you have learned. Ask Him to help you not to forget the Chapters and help you to apply them to your life!

As there are a lot of scriptures in this last Chapter, you will not find a lot of surrounding text, as in other Chapters. If you are not familiar with any scripture passage, please be sure you take your Bible and look up some surrounding text. This is to ensure the question is answered within its proper context. As usual, read the following scriptures and answer the questions.

> Isaiah 29:10 For YeHoVaH hath poured out upon you the spirit of deep sleep, and hath closed your eyes: the prophets and your rulers, the seers hath he covered. 11 And the vision of all is become unto you as the words of a book that is sealed, which [men] deliver to one that is learned, saying, Read this, I pray thee: and he saith, I cannot; for it [is] sealed: 12 And the book is delivered to him that is not learned, saying, Read this, I pray thee: and he saith, I am not learned. 13 Wherefore the Lord said, Forasmuch as this people draw near [me] with their mouth, and with their lips do honour me, but have removed their heart far from me, and their fear toward me is taught by the precept of men: 14 Therefore, behold, I will proceed to do a marvellous work among this people, [even] a marvellous work and a wonder: for the wisdom of their wise [men] shall perish, and the understanding of their prudent [men] shall be hid."

SECTION 2 — WATCHING. WAITING. WARNING. — Armed & Ready

1.	Comment:	You did this scripture in greater detail in Chapter 7. Due to its importance, it is here again for review.
	Question:	What did God pour out? (vs 10)
	Answer:	
2.	Question:	What happened to the prophets, rulers and seers?
	Answer:	
3.	Question:	How do you think this affects the people?
	Answer:	
4.	Question:	How is the vision of the Lord perceived? (vs 11-12)
	Answer:	
5.	Question:	What does verse 13 say?
	Answer:	
6.	Question:	What does God say He'll do in verse 14?
	Answer:	

7.	Question:	What happens to the wisdom of their wise men? (vs 14)	
	Answer:		
8.	Question:	What happens to the understanding of their prudent men? (vs 14)	
	Answer:		
9.	Question:	Do you perceive this verse 14 as applicable to today's generation of religious people? Explain your reasoning with scripture!	
	Answer:		

Matthew 13: 15 For this people's heart is waxed gross, and [their] ears are dull of hearing, and their eyes they have closed; lest at any time they should see with [their] eyes, and hear with [their] ears, and should understand with [their] heart, and should be converted, and I should heal them."
10.	Question:	What does Yeshua say about the people in this verse?

	Answer:	
11.	Question:	Linking this with Isaiah 29:10-14, do you see any connection with the two verses? Don't forget to explain your reasoning!
	Answer:	

Hebrews 5:10 ¶ Called of God an high priest after the order of Melchisedec. 11 Of whom we have many things to say, and hard to be uttered, seeing ye are dull of hearing."		
12.	Comment:	This passage refers to Yeshua as a great High priest, not after the order of Levi, but rather after the order of a King and priest named Melchisedec.
	Question:	In verse 11 the author says that more cannot be said, at this point. Why?
	Answer:	

Prayer Book Assignment

13.	Question:	What do you think is it like for the speaker who brings a message to those dull of hearing?
	Answer:	
14.	Question:	Looking at your answer to the previous question, why do you think it is that way?
	Answer:	

Acts 20: 28 Take heed therefore unto yourselves, and to all the flock, over the which the Holy Ghost hath made you overseers, to feed the church of God, which he hath purchased with his own blood. 29 For I know this, that after my departing shall grievous wolves enter in among you, not sparing the flock. 30 Also of your own selves shall men arise, speaking perverse things, to draw away disciples after them. 31 Therefore watch, and remember, that by the space of three years I ceased not to warn every one night and day with tears."

15.	Question:	This letter contains warnings. List those warnings in the space below.

	Answer:	

Hebrews 10: 28 He that despised Moses' law died without mercy under two or three witnesses: 29 Of how much sorer punishment, suppose ye, shall he be thought worthy, who hath trodden under foot the Son of God, and hath counted the blood of the covenant, wherewith he was sanctified, an unholy thing, and hath done despite unto the Spirit of grace? 30 For we know him that hath said, Vengeance [belongeth] unto me, I will recompense, saith the Lord. And again, The Lord shall judge his people. 31 [It is] a fearful thing to fall into the hands of the living God."

16.	Question:	What happened to those who despised the law of Moses? (vs 28)
	Answer:	
17.	Question:	Verse 29 describes an ungrateful person in the new Covenant. Describe that person.
	Answer:	

Prayer Book Assignment

18.	Question:	Shall that person escape a punishment? (vs 29)
	Answer:	
19.	Question:	What does verse 30 say about God?
	Answer:	
20.	Question:	Describe what verse 31 relates to believers.
	Answer:	
21.	Question:	Have you ever thought of that aspect of God as described in verse 31? Why or why not?
	Answer:	
22.	Question:	Do you think verse 31 applies to born again (New Covenant) believers? Explain your reasoning.
	Answer:	

Proverbs 16: 6 By mercy and truth iniquity is purged: and by the fear of YeHoVaH [men] depart from evil."

23.	Question:	By what is iniquity purged?
	Answer:	
24.	Question:	By what do people depart from evil?
	Answer:	
25.	Question:	Go to a Strong's Concordance. Write out the meaning of the word "fear". (Strong's Hebrew # 3374 (which is from 3373, which is from 3372.)
	Answer:	
26.	Question:	Christianity normally teaches that word "fear" means respect. Do you see that meaning in the Hebrew word?
	Answer:	
27.	Question:	Do you really think, if people "respect the Lord", it is enough to cause them to depart from evil? Explain your reasoning.

	Answer:	

Galatians 2: 20 I am crucified with Christ: nevertheless I live; yet not I, but Christ liveth in me: and the life which I now live in the flesh I live by the faith of the Son of God, who loved me, and gave himself for me."		
28	Question:	What does this verse say?
	Answer:	
29.	Question:	How does it apply to your life?
	Answer:	

30. Do you think a believer today, who God has called as a watchman, has a responsibility to warn others? Explain your reasoning.

31. What do you think it would take for a watchman to speak out and warn someone?

32. If you were that watchman, how would you want people to treat your warning?

33. From your Bible knowledge, do you know of any watchmen to whom the people listened? If so, why, and if not, why not?

34. As a believer, right at this moment in your spiritual life with God, do you think you are "awake" or "asleep"? Explain why you think that way.

35. In review of this course, write out what qualities you have learned that make a good watchman.

PRECIOUS MOMENTS RECAP

36.	QUESTION:	Review this workbook chapter. Pick out the scriptures that spoke to you the most. Write at least one of those scriptures in the space below.
	ANSWER:	
37.	QUESTION:	What specific truth from the scriptures you studied in this workbook chapter speaks to you. Write that truth in the space below.
	ANSWER:	

		(continue your answer here)
38.	QUESTION:	Think of how you can apply this scripture to your life. Enter those thoughts in the space below.
	39. ANSWER:	

PRAYER BOOK ASSIGNMENT

Turn to the Prayer Book. Find the Section entitled, "Warning – A Watchman's Armoury." In that section you will find an introduction and four prayers, with an explanation of that prayer.

    62. Read the Introduction. Summarize the Introduction and the scriptures that spoke to you in the space below.

    63. Read "Prayer for an Evangelist". Summarize the prayer and the scriptures that spoke to you in the provided space.

64. Read "Prayer for A Government". Summarize the prayer and the scriptures that spoke to you in the provided space.

65. Read "Prayer for Israel". Summarize the prayer and the scriptures that spoke to you in the provided space.

Prayer Book Assignment

66. Read "Prayer to Remove the Spirit of Haman". Summarize the "About the prayer" in the provided space.

67. Read "The Prayer (for removing the spirit of Haman)". Summarize the prayer and the scriptures that spoke to you in the provided space.

CONCLUSION

Open the textbook and find the page with the Heading, Personal Conclusion[31].

In the space below, recap the author's comments. Next, write down some strategical things you might do to implement your behaviour as your express your life through:

WATCHING. WAITING. WARNING.

EXTRAS FOR THE COURSE:
There are some free downloads available to help your prayer life. Go to **www.ceguallahpublishing.ca.** Look for Boot Camp Drills, Yeshua's Prayer Outline to help with this course! These and more you will find under Free Downloads! Blessings.

---

[31] When this book was written, it was on page 165. However, sometimes pages shift if some corrections are made, or even at times, when converted to pdf.

APPENDIX

If you wish to learn more about the Hebrew Alphabet, there are many online helps to teach you. On our website, you will find a PowerPoint which gives you the basics. Enter Hebrew Alphabet into the search engine or follow the QR code

HEBREW ALPHABET (WITH NUMBER, HEBREW CHARACTER, NAME OF THE LETTER, PRONUNCIATION, AND POSSIBLE MEANING.)

#	Character	Name	Pronunciation	Possible Meaning
1	א	Aleph	Ah, eh	(Ox) first or strong leader such as a father. Suggests strength to carry burdens.
2	ב	Bet	b-bh-v	(Tent) as a person's body, or a group of people such as a family, a nation.
3	ג	Gimmel	g	(foot) walking and along the same line, a person's gait (walk)
4	ד	Dalet	d	(tent door) an entrance into some places such as a doorway, or pathway or an entrance of some kind
5	ה	Heh	h, ah	(man arms outstretched) Take note, look at this. Also, God's breath is there, God has done it. Can also mean to have victory in battle) or the opposite, to surrender
6	ו	Vav (waw)	W, o, u	(nail) to join or put together, to attach, fasten,
7	ז	Zayin	z	(Plow) cut the ground or to go deep inside, penetrate
8	ח	Chet (het)	hk	(tent wall) separate, fence out, put outside, divide, wall out, keep away, resist, etc.
9	ט	Tet	t	(snake in a basket) suggests something hidden, could be a trap or snare, something lurking in the background, or could suggest a womb
10	י	Yad, yod	Y, ee	(arm & hand) could mean friendship, or the act of working or reaching out.
20	כ	Kaf	K, kh	(Open Palm of Hand) to bless, to subdue, or the hand can also beat relentlessly & wound as in the word for smitten

© CP & AA (from FMM 2010) (for more detailed information be sure to refer to Dr. Frank Seekins, Hebrew Word Pictures ISBN 9780967972619)

30	ל	Lamed	l	(shepherd's staff) authority, control, pull toward, protect, or perhaps correct
40	מ	Mem	m	(waves of the sea) waters of life, chaos, instability, even oppression
50	נ	Noon	n	(seed) as that which carries on life, so therefore could suggest inheritance
60	ס	Samekh	s	(hand on staff) to lean, to support, hold up, or could mean to rebuke or correct with a rod
70	ע	Ayin	ng	(eye to see) watch over, to see, to recognize or to become aware of something
80	פ	Pey	p, ph	(mouth) door of the person is their lips, suggests talking, perhaps the words of the mouth
90	צ	Tsade	ts	(man on side) sleep, rest, perhaps to be overpowered or in intercession as Ezekiel on side
100	ק	Qof	q	(sun on horizon) that which is past (behind you), tomorrow, sunset, or perhaps the end or beginning of a thing
200	ר	Resh	r	(head) Above, supreme, to rule
300	ש	Shin	sh	(two front teeth) East, devour, destroy, perhaps to tear to pieces, rebuke, reproof, overpower or overcome
400	ת	Tav	t	(crossed sticks) the end, or a person's mark, or sign of a covenant, perhaps the last word

© CP & AA (from FMM 2010) (for more detailed information be sure to refer to Dr. Frank Seekins, Hebrew Word Pictures ISBN 9780967972619)

SCRIPTURE REFERENCE

1

1 Corinthians 16:13	103
1 Corinthians 6: 19-20	180
1 John 2: 1-6	164
1 John 2:14-17	110
1 Kings 11:1-14	77
1 Kings 11:31-38	79
1 Kings 14:7-10	81
1 Kings 3: 7-14	75
1 Kings 3:14	77
1 Peter 4:1-7	72
1 Peter 5: 8	74
1 Peter 5:8	104
1 Samuel 13:13	42
1 Thessalonians 5:10	104
1 Thessalonians 5:6	104

2

2 Chronicles 16:9	92
2 Chronicles 20: 15-22	175
2 Corinthians 10: 1-6	173
2 Corinthians 10:1a 3-7 a	25
2 Peter 3: 11-14	137
2 Peter 3: 9-10	136
2 Peter 3:13	139
2 Timothy 2: 15-19	165
2 Timothy 2: 3-7	92

A

Acts 13:22	83
Acts 17:23	33
Acts 20: 28-31	219
Acts 20:31	103

C

Colossians 4:2	104

D

Deuteronomy 11:22	34
Deuteronomy 4:5-9	41

E

Ephesians 1: 13-14	169
Ephesians 6: 13	65
Ephesians 6:11-12	64
Ephesians 6:14-18	66
Exodus 15: 23-26	38
Exodus 15:1-3	24

G

Galatians 2: 20	223
Galatians 4: 29-30	163
Galatians 4:22-28	161
Galatians 6:1-9	117
Genesis 15	160
Genesis 15: 12-16	157

---

[32] The prayers in this book are based on many scriptures. Those included in this reference guide summarize the major scriptures used throughout the many prayers in the book.

Genesis 15: 17-21 159
Genesis 15: 7-8 154
Genesis 15: 9 159
Genesis 15: 9-11 155
Genesis 15:1 151
Genesis 15:2-6 152
Genesis 15:9 156
Genesis 17:9 38
Genesis 2:15 37
Genesis 28: 15 90
Genesis 3: 23 45
Genesis 32:28 188
Genesis 4: 10-12 127
Genesis 4: 3-7 55
Genesis 4:10-12 128
Genesis 4:9 127

H

Habakkuk 2:1-3 200
Hebrews 10: 28-31 220
Hebrews 11: 13-16 167
Hebrews 5:10-11 218

I

Isaiah 29: 7-8 184
Isaiah 29:10-14 .... 215, 218
Isaiah 29:13-14 186
Isaiah 29:7-14 187
Isaiah 29:9-12 185
Isaiah 40: 27-31 188
Isaiah 56:10-57: 1 208

J

James 1:14-15 86

James 4:1-11 116
Jeremiah 51:12 91
Joel 1: 15-2: 1 202
Joel 2:11 207
Joel 2:2-10 203
John 10: 7-10 54
John 10:1-6 53
John 14: 10 74
John 14: 28-30 71
John 14:6 12
John 15:1-8 .... 112, 177, 178
John 15:6 179

L

Luke 12:37 103
Luke 12:39 103
Luke 13:31-35 58
Luke 19:13 26
Luke 21: 7 89
Luke 21:36 89
Luke 21:8-36 89

M

Mark 13: 28-33 132
Mark 13: 34-37 134
Mark 13:34 103
Mark 13:35 103
Mark 13:37 103
Mark 14: 31-38 87
Mark 14:34 103
Mark 14:37 103
Mark 14:38 103
Matthew 13: 15 217
Matthew 22: 37-40 125

Matthew 24:42 102
Matthew 24:43 102
Matthew 25:13 102
Matthew 26:38 102
Matthew 26:40 103
Matthew 26:41 .... 103, 109

N

Nehemiah Chapter 1 47
Nehemiah Chapter 2 48
Nehemiah Chapter 3 49
Nehemiah Chapter 4 50
Numbers 6: 22-27 39
Numbers 6:24 90

P

Proverbs 10:17 43
Proverbs 16: 6 222
Psalm 119:18 53

Psalm 24:8 24
Psalm 33: 16-22 130
Psalm 36:9 199
Psalm 37:34 43
Psalm 45:3 24
Psalm 45:6 91
Psalm 47:8 91

R

Revelation 16:15 104
Revelation 19:11-16 25
Revelation 3:2 104
Revelation 3:3 104
Romans 11:1-8 182

Z

Zechariah 1:1-3 60
Zechariah 4:10 92

Cegullah Publishing & Apologetics Academy

CONTACT INFORMATION

www.cegullahpublishing.ca

Visit our website for some free downloads and helps to live your Christian life!